PEMBROKES UNDER F

C000003797

The Story of the Air Raids
of 1940-41

by
BILL RICHARDS
(Formerly Chief Reporter and South Pembrokeshire
representative of the West Wales Guardian who lived in
Pembroke Dock at the time of the air raids).

First published in book form by the West Wales Guardian:
June,1965.
Second Edition: July, 1965.
Third Edition: October, 1983
Fourth Edition, with minor text amendments and additional
photographs, published by Paterchurch Publications: July, 1995.
Fifth Edition: October 2003.
Sixth Edition: April 2008

Cover design: Laurie Glover.
Printing: Colourprint UK. 01646 623700

Published by: PATERCHURCH PUBLICATIONS,
8 Laws Street, Pembroke Dock,
Pembrokeshire, SA72 6DL
Tel: 01646 683041
ISBN: 1870745 05 1

IN MEMORIAM

This book is dedicated to the memory of those defenceless civilians who lost their lives under enemy bombardment, amongst them the following :-

W. KINTON
Mrs. KINTON
Mrs. HARVEY
JAMES ALLEN
Mrs. A. R. BRAZELL
Miss K. BRAZELL
S. H. BUXTON
R. E. BURDER
Mrs. M. E. T. EVANS
Miss G. E. EVANS
T. EVANS
Mrs. E. HEATH
M. HEATH
Mrs. D. A. HEARN
Mrs. E. HUTCHINGS
E. JONES
Mrs. L. E. McKENZIE
ALEXANDER McKENZIE
Master CYRIL McKENZIE
ARTHUR KAVANAGH
J. F. HARRIES
Mrs. HARRIES
Mrs. B. H. HAMERTON

JACK BASKERVILLE
CYRIL JENKINS
Mrs. M. EVANS
W. S. POUNDER
THOMAS PHILLIPS
H. H. R. REYNOLDS
Mrs. REYNOLDS
Mrs. A. B. ROBINSON
Mrs. E. F. SAUNDERS
H. ROACH
C. G. UNDERHILL
J. H. THOMAS
Miss E. WILLIAMS
H. WILLIAMS
Mrs. E. M. EVANS
Mrs. E. GRIFFITHS
Miss E. GRIFFITHS
R. MORRIS
Miss E. MORRIS
Mrs. G. THOMAS
R. . LENHAM
Mrs. LENHAM and child

(The above should not be taken as a complete list of those killed in the Pembrokeshire air raids).

CONTENTS

INTRODUCTION

Most of the material in this book appeared in a series of articles by the Author in the county newspaper, the *West Wales Guardian*, in 1945, soon after the end of World War II. It was then possible for the first time, the censorship restrictions having been lifted, to give all the facts of the air raids in the county and to tell the full story of the heroism, the humour, pathos and tragedy which went hand-in-hand during those grim days.

Because of the great interest shown, especially in Pembroke Dock - the target of much of the enemy action - the articles were later published in book form. It was felt that in addition to meeting a popular demand, this would provide a permanent record of a critical period in the life of the county.

The book was sold out within a month of publication in 1965 and, with requests for copies coming in from all parts of the country, it was quickly reprinted. A new edition was printed in 1983 and continued to sell all over the country and to Pembrokeshire 'exiles' all over the world. It has also been used as a textbook for schools.

In 1995, with the full consent of the Author, the copyright passed to Paterchurch Publications of Pembroke Dock and a new edition was published in the 50th anniversary year of the end of World War 11. The text remained virtually unchanged but many additional photographs of special historic appeal were added.

Demand for *Pembrokeshire Under Fire* continues and this sixth edition has been printed to meet that demand.

Bill Richards, who served Pembrokeshire loyally in so many ways, especially as a journalist on the *West Wales Guardian* for over 50 years, as an author of several local books and as a JP, died in January 2003, aged 88.

BY THE SAME AUTHOR
The Schoolmaster Abroad
Everyone for Tennis Jointly)
Lives of Great Men....
A Well-found Ship
The County Hospital Story
Faith, Hope and Fairways
Changing face of Haverfordwest
Haverfordwest My Grandstand

HEADS IN THE SAND

At about 2 o'clock on Friday afternoon, July 5th, 1940, an air raid siren sounded in Pembroke Dock. No Air Raid Precautions practice had been announced and people came to their doors in hundreds to stare up into the sky. There was nothing to be seen. "It must be another practice", they said and began to talk about the weather and other more interesting topics. The following day a few lines tucked away in an obscure corner of a daily paper read, "Yesterday enemy 'planes approached the Welsh coast but turned back before crossing inland". Those who put two and two together were satisfied that the previous day's siren was the first air raid warning to be sounded in earnest in Pembrokeshire - and the full import of it did not escape them. But to an amazingly large number of people in Pembrokeshire there was just "nothing to it". The Germans were in France, which put the all-powerful Luftwaffe within easy striking distance of any place in Wales. Pembrokeshire had many valuable military targets which the enemy would be quite justified in striking. But somehow the vast majority of people seemed convinced that Pembrokeshire would never hear a bomb explode. "The German airmen will have bigger fish to fry, they will attack the bigger cities" - that was the sort of statement with which we were re-assured, and, it cannot be denied, there was some comfort to be found in such predictions.

Thus it was that when the siren sounded for the first time without warning most people just could not believe it meant the real thing. The refusal of the townspeople of Pembroke Dock to take that Friday afternoon warning seriously was such that the *West Wales Guardian* felt constrained to comment upon it as follows:- "On a certain afternoon recently an air raid warning was sounded in a certain town (**the censor was then at the height of his power!**). At the time there was no reason to think the siren was anything other than a genuine warning of the approach of enemy aircraft. But did the people of the town act as if this were so? They did not. Did they drop the work - or pleasure - of the moment and hurry to whatever shelter could be found? They did not. Did parents whose children had been sent running home from school for safety see that those children were kept indoors or sent to a place of safety? They did not. Did trains, buses, lorries, cars come to a standstill ready for the worst? They did not. Instead, a scene of the most astounding complacency was witnessed ... This is not bravery. It is nothing but crass stupidity". The *Guardian* warned people that air raids were a distinct possibility and that if they came they would not be an entertainment to be watched from the doorsteps. The *Guardian* was criticised for that article. It was said that the paper was scaring the people unnecessarily. Within a week Pembroke Dock had had its first air raid, and the complacent ones were beginning to revise their views.

From early July, 1940, until June, 1941, Pembrokeshire was subjected to many air raids. The good folk of the county learnt full well all the sounds of aerial battle, from the banshee wail of the siren which broke the stillness of many a fine night, to the sickening crash of exploding bombs. They learnt to

Summer days ... Pembroke Dock basks in the summer sunshine in 1938. On the water are Singapore III and Sunderland flying-boats while at top right can be seen the RAF floating dock, nicknamed locally as 'HMS Flat Iron'. This photograph was taken from a RAF flying-boat stationed at Pembroke Dock. Just two years later black-crossed Luftwaffe bombers would have a similar view of the dockyard town.

Group Captain H. D. Newman

recognise the discordant note of approaching enemy bombers; they learnt to distinguish between bomb explosions and anti-aircraft fire; they became familiar with the rattle of machine guns, the weaving pattern of the searchlights, the grim beauty of an anti-aircraft barrage, the ghostly sound of falling incendiaries, the smell of cordite, the crashing of glass, the rumble of falling masonry, and the dread thud of parachute mines striking down. Worst of all, they suffered the loss of many relatives and friends who gave their lives under a merciless bombardment. Throughout the period Pembroke Dock was the centre of the attack. While important places like Milford Haven and Trecwn escaped practically unscathed, Pembroke Dock - long a Cinderella in local and national affairs - received constant attention. It was the most trying period in the town's history, a period when the townspeople lived on the edge of their nerves and went about with jumpy step and drawn, anxious faces. It is useless to try and disguise the fact that morale reached a low ebb. The people were scared and where is there a reasonable man or woman who will blame them? Perhaps, even today, it is not fully appreciated that the damage inflicted in Pembroke Dock was as great as that in any blitzed town in the country - every house in the place was damaged to some extent - while the death roll for one raid was as high in proportion as that of most of the big towns. In fact, it was considerably higher than that of many towns whose suffering in the blitz received world-wide publicity.

HAVEN'T WE GOT ANY DEFENCES?

Wednesday, July 10th, 1940, will live for ever in Pembrokeshire's history for it was on that day that the County took the first shock of an enemy air attack. The air raid itself, carried out by a solitary 'plane, was a very minor affair compared with what was to come, but it will probably be remembered as much as any, simply because it was the first. It came like a bolt from the blue (literally!); it was an event which in some degree at least, had never been seriously anticipated locally, an event which in the few violent minutes of its duration changed the war from something which one read about in the newspapers to an immediate and frightening menace to home and loved ones. Its impact upon the local mind was such that now, when many of the other air raids have become a dim memory, residents of Pembroke Dock, where the bombs fell, still say, "But that was the day, that Wednesday when Jerry made his first raid..."

It was cloudy and overcast that Wednesday morning, the ideal day for a

Practice ... During what proved to be the last Empire Air Day at RAF Pembroke Dock - in May, 1939 - an 'ARP display' was staged for the large crowd. Against the backdrop of Llanion Barracks and Pier Road smoke rises following a small explosion. Peacetime practice was to lead to wartime reality in 1940 and 1941.

Group Captain Guy Bolland

sneak raid. Pembroke Dock had gone about its work in the usual way. The flying boats in the dockyard and out in the harbour could be heard revving-up as usual, the familiar sound interspersed occasionally by the high roaring note of the Dutch seaplanes recently arrived after the invasion of the Netherlands. Then it came. At precisely 10.12 a.m. without any warning, the whole town was rocked by a terrific explosion. There had been no siren and in those days an air raid without warning was unthinkable (how we were to learn!). All the same in many shops and offices workers looked at each other, a trifle pale, and murmured "Bombs". Minutes passed and nothing happened. The sound of not even one aircraft could be heard. Perhaps it wasn't a bomb after all? People began to venture into the street, craning their necks. No, there was not an aircraft to be seen.

"It's O.K. There's been an explosion down in the workshops on the Pier Road", said an unconcerned gentleman walking along Bush Street. But that convinced no one and for several minutes animated conversations about the meaning of it all were continued on the pavements. Then, at 10.20, all speculation was ended-by the sounding of the siren in the R.A.F. Station. It was an air raid all right. A few minutes later the raider came in again across the town. There it was for all to see, a big, black Junkers 88, flying from east to west, high and close to the heavy blanket of cloud. I had ventured, albeit with extreme caution, from the *Guardian* Office as far as the Bird in Hand in Lewis Street, and from the pavement there watched the 'plane in company with the genial landlord, Alderman Joe Gibby. As we watched, two black specks appeared beneath the 'plane. "Birds," said I, with more hope than conviction. "Birds be d-d". exclaimed Ald. Gibby, a veteran of 1914-18, "They're bombs, come on in". The explosions did not seem quite so terrifying from a crouching position beside the bar! Two stiff whiskies a few moments later (out of hours) did much to restore the equilibrium of both of us!

During the next few minutes there were further explosions, between which machine-gun fire was heard - coming from the Barrack Hill where some soldiers were "having a go" at the intruder. At the time many people feared the streets were being machine-gunned. In all the excitement the sounding of the town siren - about twenty minutes late - went almost unnoticed. Some ten minutes later the Junkers flew away down south to return to its base, where, according to a later German news bulletin, the pilot reported "a heavy raid on Pembroke where large fires were started".

Actually, the damage caused by this raider, in what must have been one of the easiest assignments any bomber crew could ever have had, was infinitesimal. The first bomb which so shook the town fell in the harbour between Neyland and Pembroke Dock. It must have been a big bomb, its detonation being as great as any experienced in subsequent raids apart, of course, from that of the landmines on May 12th, 1941. Had it fallen in the town it would doubtless have wreaked tremendous havoc. As it was, it was a very near thing. Had the bomb fallen a few hundred yards to the south-east it would have hit Llanion Barracks and might have blown up the powder magazine ! Furthermore, the ferry-boat with a full complement of passengers had just passed within a few yards of where the bomb hit the water! People at Hobbs Point and the Neyland pontoon were dazed by the explosion. Shrapnel fell all around them, particularly at Hobbs Point, but miraculously no one was hit. The only casualties were scores of fish which, killed or stunned by the explosion, came to the surface and were washed ashore to provide many a tasty meal for the people living in the Llanion area. The other bombs, four or five in number and of smaller calibre, fell in and around Llanreath. The enemy was evidently after the oil tanks and although it was not generally known at the time, one bomb found its mark. But luck was with Pembroke Dock that day and the tank did not blow up. The bomb must have been a dud ! Evidence of the raider's marksmanship was provided by a neat hole in the top of one of the tanks. Delayed action bombs being little heard of in those days, many people climbed a ladder to examine the cavity – and, months later, shivered at the very thought of it!

This air raid, the first of many, was the sole topic of conversation in Pembroke Dock that day and for several days afterwards. To the rest of the county it was a matter of great interest but to the Borough of Pembroke it was one of vital concern. Pembroke Dock became really A.R.P.-conscious over night and braced itself to meet a grim period ahead. The townspeople were taken aback by the air raid itself but there was far greater concern at the almost complete defencelessness of the area and the fact that the siren was so late giving warning. Apart from a few rounds fired from a machine-gun, the raider had had the sky to itself and had carried out the bombing in safety and at leisure. The attitude of the townspeople was summed up by a well-known local professional gentleman when he remarked the following day: "That pilot was a Jerry but he must have been a gentleman to have stuck to military objectives. There was nothing to stop him machine-gunning and bombing the town. Haven't we got any defences?" We were soon to learn by grim experience that anti-aircraft defences in Pembrokeshire were almost non existent and that the system of warning was to take many months to become efficient. In fact, during those early days bombs-before-siren was the rule. By the time the siren became of any use the enemy was beginning to switch his attentions elsewhere.

NO HOPE OF GUNS -
BUT THE PUBLIC DIDN'T KNOW!

Pembroke Dock was given only a few days to recover from the shock of its first air raid. On Monday, July 15th, 1940, the enemy made his second visit. Shortly after noon the Air Station siren was sounded and the people, with the previous Wednesday very much in mind, went to their shelters. A little later a 'plane could be heard, flying very high, but, if it was the enemy, it must have continued on its way, for the all-clear went without event. An hour afterwards, however, when most people had just finished their lunch, a noisy 'plane was heard coming in low across the town, followed in a few seconds by three or four explosions in quick succession. Then there was a burst of machine-gun fire, and after that - silence. Again the siren had failed. The bombs had exploded and the intruder was well on his way out of the locality before its eerie note was heard, and then it was the siren belonging to the R.A.F. The town's public siren came into its own half-an-hour later to sound the all-clear.

While the raid of the previous Wednesday was obviously carried out according to a carefully prepared plan this one appeared to be a "pot shot" effort by a pilot who happened to be passing near Pembroke Dock. The bombs fell in the field by the Birdcage Walk and did no damage. They were probably aimed at the railway bridge over Ferry Lane or at the railway line itself. In either case it was a pretty poor attempt and local people began to place some credence upon the oft-repeated story that Jerry was a wretched shot. What the machine-gun fire was directed at it is difficult to conjecture, but it was sufficient to make Ald. Joe Gibby (previously mentioned in this story) think for a while that the Germans were conducting a personal vendetta against him! Ald. Gibby was strolling along the Birdcage Walk with his dogs when the bombs whistled down followed in a few seconds by the machine-gun bullets which spattered around him. He fell on his face and, by great good fortune, escaped any injury.

The public concern at the failure of the siren was evidenced by letters which appeared in the *West Wales Guardian* on the following Thursday. Ald. J. R. Williams stated that the knowledge that bombs might drop on the town at any time without any warning had caused a great deal of uneasiness. He complained that while the town siren had sounded the all-clear after the R.A.F. siren, it had failed to follow the R.A.F. in giving the warning. "Few", he stated, "can understand an arrangement whereby the local A.R.P. officials follow the example of another authority (the R.A.F.) in giving an all-clear but fail to do so with regard to the more important warning that an air raid is imminent. If it is true that the local officials have to wait authority from elsewhere before sounding the warning it is time there was a drastic revision of arrangements. Surely every town should be allowed to act on its own initiative?" In another letter, signed by C. A. Lockett and E. G. Channon, 17 Waterloo, complaint was made that the siren was not loud enough to be

Silver lady ... A majestic Sunderland flying-boat, still in peacetime silver, lies at a mooring off the RAF Station, Pembroke Dock. The flying-boat station, and the naval and army installations in and around the town, made Pembroke Dock a very legitimate military target. This Sunderland - L2167 of 210 Squadron - was lost near Oslo, Norway, in April, 1940, after the German invasion of that country.

John Evans Collection

heard in all parts of the town and that there was a deplorable lack of air raid shelters. These matters were for weeks the subject of urgent representations by Pembroke Dock to the powers that be. The trouble over the sounding of the siren reached a climax a little later when Ald. Williams put it off on his own initiative and was afterwards threatened with dire punishment, including imprisonment! Further details of that interesting occurrence will be given later. There was equal, if not greater concern, at the apparent ease with which the Germans were allowed to carry out their raids. The position and the local attitude towards it were aptly summed up in the following lines by "Camelot" which appeared in the *Guardian* of June 19th, 1940:-

NOT A GUN WAS FIRED!

Not a gun was fired, not an airplane rose,
When the bombs round the old town were popping:
Not an air raid warden showed his nose
While the missiles were leisurely dropping;
Calmly, unhurriedly fared the Hun,
From the field of his task as a vandal;
But for paralysed 'plane and silent gun-
Oh ! Whom shall we blame for the scandal ?

The uneasiness of the townspeople was reflected at the meetings of the Borough Council where demands were made for defences for the area, for the scheduling of Pembroke Dock as a danger zone so that Anderson shelters could be obtained with Government assistance, and for the provision of detector plates to be erected in the town so that poison gases could be identified if used by the enemy. The Council took various steps, amongst other things writing to the then County M.P. (Major Gwilym Lloyd George) regarding the defences of the area. On Saturday, July 20th, Major Lloyd George visited the Borough and attended a special meeting of the Council at the Town Hall, Pembroke. What Major Gwilym told the Council that Saturday morning could not be disclosed at the time. He said that because of the tremendous losses at Dunkirk the whole country, including many important war factories, etc., was practically defenceless, and Pembroke would have to wait for a very long time before it had any guns. For national security reasons, even a hint at this disturbing news in the Press was out of the question, although the local reporters were taken fully into the confidence of the Council and were present throughout the vital discussion with Major Lloyd George. If the information had been made known its effect, taking the purely local aspect, would have been almost disastrous. The news rather took the wind out of the sails of the Council, including the worthy Mayor, Clr. John Gwyther, who had complained in no uncertain terms to Major Lloyd George that German 'planes should be permitted to fly around Pembroke of all places without anyone to say them nay! But the members took it well and assured the Major that the morale of the Borough was of the highest. "We have not got the wind up here at all", Ald. W. J. Gwilliam told him. "In fact our tails are well up". That, of course, was the right thing to say at the time, but Ald. Gwilliam must have had his tongue in his cheek. Perhaps he was thinking of Pembroke rather than of Pembroke Dock!

At that meeting it was decided to urge the County Council to delegate powers to the local authority so that the matter of air raid shelters, etc., could be proceeded with without delay. It was also decided that Mr. Kavanagh, the engineer, should carry out an inspection of houses for the purpose of strengthening domestic air raid shelters.

FIRST NIGHT ATTACK

Nowadays, one might be thought guilty of exaggeration in saying that the most acute apprehension existed in Pembroke Dock as long, sunny days marked the opening of the holiday month in 1940. Such is human nature that bombing has already become a faint memory. But it was something real, near, terrifying and all important in those dark days. So let no one look back now and say that the people who were frightened of the bombs in 1940 were showing the white feather. They were not, they were merely human. Remember that these were civilians without that disciplinary training which becomes of such incalculable value to the Serviceman when the hour of battle arrives; civilians who had not expected war on their doorsteps, who in common with the whole country were aghast and alarmed at the general development of the war, and who knew that when the enemy came they could do little but sit and "wait for it". That was their position. Mr. Churchill was promising the country blood and toil and tears and sweat and saying that revenge upon the Germans would not come until 1942 and 1943, which seemed an interminable time to wait. Truly, the years stretched before us, bleak, cheerless and frightening. Pembroke Dock had had two air raids. It was obvious that greater trials lay ahead.

It was not long before they came. On July 22nd, a week after the attempted bombing (presumably) of the Ferry Lane railway bridge, the ex-dockyard town experienced its first night raid. It was a Monday night and there was a clear, star-studded sky with little breeze. Most of the law-abiding citizens of Pembroke Dock had gone to bed and were about to go off to sleep when, just before midnight, the siren sounded. Its wailing note, disconcerting enough in broad daylight, seemed a real harbinger of trouble as it pierced the silence of the night. People scrambled to shelter, and only just in time for within two minutes a 'plane could be heard. Its droning grew louder, until it was over the town. There were those incurable optimists who from the depths of their cellars proclaimed it to be "one of ours chasing them off".

Then there was another sound. It began as a whisper and rapidly grew into a sharp, shrieking whistle which ripped the air like the lash of a giant whip. The whole town shivered as the bombs crashed down. Some more bombs followed, after which there was a long silence broken intermittently by the sound of aircraft overhead. At about I a.m. anxious ears again heard a 'plane approach. As they steeled themselves for the explosions which might come at any moment, no doubt many people began to persuade themselves they were getting used to it. But there was something new in store. Suddenly the droning of the 'plane was drowned by the most unearthly shriek. It started low and rose in a petrifying crescendo as if all the fiends of hell were coming screaming to earth on forked lightning. Then there were explosions. Pembroke Dock had heard its first screaming bombs. It is difficult to describe adequately to someone who has never heard one what a screaming bomb is really like. It has the effect of making all persons within miles of it think it is falling right on top of them personally. It was produced as a

Target ... An aerial view of part of the newly established RAF Carew Cheriton air station, showing the World War One vintage canvas hangars first used there. This photograph, dating from 1939, was taken before the runways were constructed. RAF Carew Cheriton was subjected to a number of Luftwaffe raids.

Deric Brock Collection

weapon of terror and that it certainly was.

The "screamers" were the last to fall in the Pembroke Dock vicinity that night, and after another quiet spell the all-clear sounded at about 2 a.m. People turned in and went to sleep, thankful to be still alive and feeling secure now that the raid was over. They did not know that throughout that night "yellow" messages were being received at County A.R.P. headquarters and that it was nearly noon on the following day before the last "white" (all clear) came through! According to one report, at least eighteen bombs were dropped that night; probably, there were several more. One bomb dropped between Front Street and the dockyard railway causing a great deal of damage in nearby houses. Windows were shattered and flying debris smashed through roofs, while the explosion dislodged ceilings and caused large zig-zag cracks in walls. A large, gaping hole was blasted in the dividing wall between two houses in Front Street. In the house most damaged the family with friends, numbering nine altogether, sheltered beneath the staircase while the building tottered about them. They escaped unhurt.

Another bomb came down between King Street and the railway and a third exploded in the gardens between Market Street and Pembroke Street. Other bombs fell in the haven, some near the R.N. Mines Depot, and two at Hobbs Point; five exploded between Carew and Cosheston; four at West Williamston; another behind Lawrenny Castle, and two on Mr. Rock's farm at Waterston. Those bombs which fell in the open fields caused large craters, evidence that they were of fairly large calibre judged by 1940 standards.

By a miracle no one was killed or even slightly injured in this raid and on the following Sunday afternoon the townspeople held an open-air service of thanksgiving. As the Vicar (Rev. D. D. Bartlett, later Bishop of St. Asaph) in a short address, thanked God for His care and mercy, tears streamed down the faces of many of the congregation.

Meanwhile, there were three other places which had felt the fury of the attack - the adjoining villages of Carew, Sageston and Milton. Obviously the Germans were after Milton aerodrome, and for security reasons little could be said at the time of the attacks in that area. But it was plain that the enemy had a very good idea of the location of the airfield, and several attacks were made upon it, not without success. Indeed, according to one report, the biggest death roll for one air raid in Pembrokeshire was at Milton, all the casualties being servicemen. The first raid on the 'drome occurred about noon on July 19th. Seven high explosives dropped in Sageston while a number exploded on the airfield and others in fields. Three contractor's workmen were injured by bomb splinters - William Alfred Edwards, Redberth, David Richards, Saundersfoot, and Ivor Hughes, Kilgetty. There was considerable damage to property round about.

Strangely enough, a large number of people outside Pembroke, Pembroke Dock and the locality of the haven, now becoming known as the target area, remained quite complacent and unappreciative of what bombing really meant. One Haverfordwest gentleman went so far as to remark to Mr. Harry Reynolds, of Laws Street, Pembroke Dock, that he could not understand why Pembroke Dock people should be afraid of an air raid because they could always dodge the bombs if they watched them coming down! Mr. Reynolds, later killed in the heaviest raid of all, had his own picturesque way of describing-this airy-fairy attitude towards Pembroke Dock's grim plight. Deputy Chief Constable Anthony Thomas, who will long be remembered in Pembroke Dock, also had a word for the distant critics. "What they want is a few 500 pounders round their ears", he used to say. But invariably he would add a favourite expression -"Mind you, God forbid that such a thing should happen".

THE EXODUS BEGINS

After the first night raid people began to go out of the town to sleep. It started in a small way but as the raids grew in severity developed into a veritable exodus until in May, 1941, Pembroke Dock was literally depopulated at night time. Throughout the period of the raids there was sharp controversy over this question of people leaving the town. It became largely a matter of those who sought safety outside the target area being criticised by those who for a variety of reasons were unable to do so. Unfortunately the controversy was not without bitterness and there were many allegations of cowardice which were largely unfounded and which, generally speaking, were quite illogical. About this time, too, complaints were being voiced that A.R.P. workers and firemen were failing to turn out for duty, but here again the position was considerably exaggerated. In August, however, the then Fire Chief, Mr. Arthur Morris, thought it expedient to report to the Council that five members of the Auxiliary Fire Service had failed to turn out upon a "red" message. Four of the men appeared before the Council and three gave explanations which were accepted. The fourth said he had to see that his wife and children were all right. He also contended that there was insufficient protection and said frankly he was not prepared to turn out in a raid. His resignation and that of the fifth fireman, who wrote that his wife had collapsed when the warning was given, were accepted.

Of course, these men as members of the A.F.S. formed a vital part of the town's defence, such as it was, and it was of the utmost importance that they should turn out in as full strength as possible. They had a duty to perform. But the complaint that the men were not afforded sufficient protection was not entirely groundless. The fire station, situated right alongside the Air Base, was considered to be right in the bull's eye of the target; moreover, the place was not reinforced in any way at the time, while it was said that a large quantity of petrol was stored nearby. It certainly was not a healthy place for the firemen to sit and wait for a call while the Boche roared overhead. Neither must it be concluded that the firemen and the humble A.R.P. workers were the only ones who were reluctant to show themselves to be reckless heroes after the siren had warbled its eerie warning. A few months later a story was told, and there is no reason to doubt it, of a very important A.R.P. official visiting Pembroke Dock about half-an-hour after a heavy raid. He had just pulled up outside the Report Centre and was chatting to a local worker on the pavement before going inside when the siren went again. Hastily looking at his watch, the important official exclaimed, "By jove, I've just remembered I've got an appointment with Mr. Rowlands in Pembroke". And he jumped into his car and was off to the midnight rendezvous !

At a meeting of the County Council on 23rd July, the programme for the construction of public air raid shelters in the county was presented and approved. This provided a ray of hope to Pembroke Dock people, and not before time, as there was grave concern at the absence of public shelters. At one meeting of the Borough Council early in August bitter complaint was made that public shelters were almost complete in raid-free Haverfordwest while in Pembroke and Pembroke Dock the bricks were still lying about in piles, much to the delight of the children, who, according to Alderman Hay, were having great fun aiming them at each other! So strong was public feeling becoming on this question that a threat was made to organise a petition for presentation to H.M. the King protesting that the Borough was not receiving the attention it deserved! Cooler counsels prevailed before this drastic step could be put into effect, but it was decided to make urgent representations to the County Authority. Also forwarded to the County A.R.P. Committee was a petition signed by fifty-eight residents of Llanreath protesting that the siren could not be heard in the village and asking for the installation of a separate siren. As Llanreath had had first-hand experience of bombing in the first raid on July 10th, the petition was not lacking in earnestness!

Castle town ... Fears that the Norman town of Pembroke, just two miles from Pembroke Dock, had been attacked in July, 1940, were happily unfounded and the town escaped the attentions of the Luftwaffe. An Australian crewman in a Sunderland took this photograph in 1943.

Dr. Jock Rolland

After the night raid of July 22nd-23rd, there was a spell of over a week before "Jerry" made another visit. This occurred on the night of Thursday, August 1st, at about 11. 15. It was a hit-and-run attack made by a lone 'plane which dropped ten bombs across Llanion Barracks. Again the siren failed to function in time, the first intimation that the 'plane was a German being the whistling of the bombs. It was a fine summer's evening and, it having only just gone dusk, there were many people about the streets when the raid occurred. Now familiar with the heralding whine of the bombs they fell on their faces as soon as they heard it. Those who had gone to bed were awakened by the explosions and were in their cellars when the siren sounded. The all-clear sounded in about half-an-hour. Although the bombs fell right across the barracks, surprisingly little damage was done. One bomb, however, killed a soldier. The unfortunate soldier, twenty-year-old Ronald Johnston, of Manchester, was standing up at the time and was struck in the stomach by a piece of shrapnel. This was the first fatal casualty to have occurred by enemy action in the county.

Later on that night many people thought that an incendiary attack had been made on Pembroke. Awakened by a 'plane, they saw a bright red glow in the direction of Pembroke station. The 'plane could be heard droning overhead and under the conditions which then prevailed, one could be forgiven for thinking the worst. The red glow was not due to enemy action, however. It was caused by a disastrous fire which occurred at the Pembroke Motor and Electrical Engineering Works in Station Road, Pembroke. The outbreak was discovered in the early hours of the morning and continued until daybreak. Added to the anxieties of the firemen and the people living in the locality was the fear that the great blaze would attract enemy aircraft which might be in the vicinity. Indeed for a long time a 'plane could be heard high overhead and there were many anxious moments but it was later learned from a reliable source that it was one of our night fighters sent to protect the area because of the fire.

At this time German 'planes were roaming our skies almost at will and several attacks were made on Milford trawlers which were then not armed even with machine guns. Amongst the trawlers attacked were those skippered by Messrs. Edward Lewis, Eastleigh Drive, Alec Smith, Wellington Road (skipper of the "*Milford Viscount*" which disappeared on a fishing trip in April, 1950), Walter Perry, Greville Road, J. Cheyney, Point Street, Hakin, and W. Davies, Picton Road, Hakin. One ship, the s.t. "*Ermine*" was bombed and machine-gunned for twenty minutes. The bosun, Mr. Fred McKay, Prioryville, on watch on the bridge at the time, had a bullet through one knee, while the other leg was also injured. Skipper Perry and the chief engineer, Mr. George Turrell, were also slightly injured. These attacks continued and for some time the gallant fishermen could do nothing but shake their fists at the Nazi airmen - which they did in grand defiance!

THE GREAT TANKS FIRE

Pembroke Dock had not been deemed worthy of much consideration in the country's defence arrangements or even of a mention in the national news bulletins - until on Monday, August 19th, a German 'plane flew up the harbour and dropped a bomb plumb on one of the Llanreath oil tanks. The blaze which followed was one of the biggest in the history of Britain and, overnight, Pembroke Dock became an important place to our own people as well as to the Germans, who had obviously thought so all along. While the tanks blazed furiously and gallant firemen were making heroic efforts to stem the flames, anti-aircraft guns began to arrive in the locality and barrage balloons appeared in the sky over Pembroke Dock. Local people were inclined to look upon this as an attempt to close the stable door after the

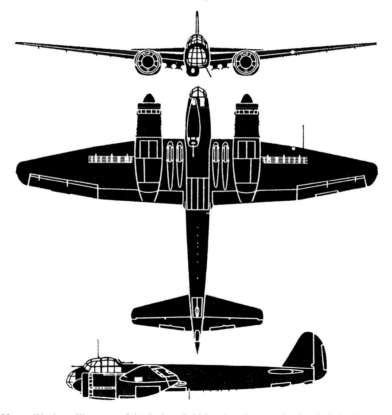

Raider ... Wartime silhouettes of the Junkers Ju88 bomber, the type that bombed the Llanreath oil tanks in August, 1940. The raid was carried out by three Ju 88s of Kampfgruppe 51, the famous Edelweiss Squadron then based near Paris. A very versatile aircraft, the Ju 88 saw service with the German forces throughout the war.

Via Laurie Glover

horse had gone, but, nevertheless, they were grateful for the defences, which remained to protect the area a great deal in future raids. A short time afterwards a start was made on the building of concrete walls to protect the oil tanks at Llanion, but strangely enough, as far as one was able to judge the raiders' actions, these tanks were not made a specific target in subsequent attacks.

In the meanwhile the Germans were making the most of their success in setting the tanks on fire. They described it as a great success by the Luftwaffe, and for once they were telling the truth. It was a serious blow to Britain's war effort, probably the most serious of the early air raids. The fire destroyed an immense quantity of precious heavy oil and, at one time, threatened to set the whole town on fire. Lord Haw Haw did not forget to gloat over these facts and to add a few dire threats about far more terrible things to come. But he did not say that the German airmen's success was easily achieved, that the raid was made without opposition apart from R.A.F. fighter 'planes which at the time were deplorably few even in areas far more important than Pembrokeshire. The Germans gave a great build-up to the pilot of the aircraft which bombed the tanks. They said that he was only a lad of sixteen but was a skilful and daring pilot, who had accomplished many successful raids on Britain. The report added that the young pilot had failed to return to base and it was presumed that he had died for his Fuehrer. This was probably the truth because after the attack a report gained currency locally that Spitfires had chased the raiders out to sea where one of them was shot down.

The raid occurred about 3.15 on the Monday afternoon and was made by three aircraft. They flew up the harbour very low and in quite leisurely fashion, turning south before reaching Pembroke Dock and then coming in again to approach the tanks from the direction of Monkton. Not a gun was fired at them, although there is a reliable report that some gunners in the Milford area were positively itching to shoot but were unable to do so without orders. Up at the tanks, workmen engaged on trenching looked up at the approaching 'planes and thinking they were British bent over their tools again. Then the bomber dived in and the men ran for shelter. Fire bombs were dropped and a hit was obtained on a tank holding 12,000 tons of oil. A great tongue of flame shot up and clouds of black, thick, oily smoke billowed high into the sky. Within seconds it was obvious for many miles around that the tanks were burning. People living in Haverfordwest heard the explosion and, seeing the great mass of smoke and flames, guessed what had happened. By great good fortune the workmen at the tanks escaped without injury and the raid itself did not cause a single casualty although Mr. Fred Phillips, Pennar, had to be treated in hospital for shock. The people living in Military Road right alongside the tanks had a severe shaking and looked on in alarm as the wind carried flames and great volumes of smoke in the direction of their homes. Their alarm was well justified. For nearly three weeks they were to live alongside a terrifying inferno which allowed no rest day or night.

Black out ... 'vast clouds of smoke blacked out the summer sky ...' – a photograph taken on the Barrack Hill.

Roy Hordley

The constant roaring of the flames became to these people a devil's chant. The vast clouds of smoke blacked out the summer sky and the fire turned the nights into a lurid hell. The walls of some of the houses became too hot to touch and the oil-laden smoke percolated into many rooms leaving a trail of ruin. To all of Pembroke Dock those three weeks formed a period of great anxiety but no residents suffered as much as those in Military Road and Pennar generally. Many of them, especially from amongst the older people, moved to other parts of the town or out of the town altogether, but a large number remained and they were deserving of the highest praise for sticking it out. Some who feared that the fire would spread during the night and set the street alight took to leaving their houses when darkness fell and snatching as much sleep as they could out on the Barrack Hill. Probably another reason for this was that they felt safer there from further air attacks.

Within a few minutes of the attack the Pembroke Dock Fire Brigade was on the scene and, under Mr. Arthur Morris, gallantly tackled what they knew was going to be a colossal task. Meanwhile messages were flashed to all parts of the county and soon several brigades were speeding to join in the great task. The Pembroke and Pembroke Dock brigades performed wonderful work before other brigades arrived. They were largely responsible for preventing the flames spreading to the nearby houses. They were on the scene before the raiders had cleared off when there might be another shower of bombs at any moment. They held the fire for several hours. Yet when the bouquets were handed out after it was all over the local men got scarcely a mention.

GALLANTRY AWARDS
CAUSE A STORM

The tanks fire raged in full fury for eighteen days. During that period over six hundred firemen from all parts of the country fought the flames; eleven tanks each with a capacity of 12,000 tons were destroyed; five firemen lost their lives; the enemy made further savage but fruitless attacks, and the whole town and countryside bore traces of oil carried by the smoke which billowed far and wide. Auxiliary firemen from all parts of the county were on the scene a few hours after the attack and within the next two or three days they were re-inforced by brigades from Carmarthen, Swansea, Cardiff, Bristol, Birmingham, Newport and other parts of the country. Altogether twenty-two brigades took part in the colossal task. These men faced one of the grimmest fights of their lives. No battlefield ever presented a more ghastly picture. Flames sprang hundreds of feet into the air and, every few minutes, shot outwards treacherously from the tanks in great enveloping sheets; the heat was overpowering and the smoke blinding, choking, stupefying. Yet the firemen stuck to their task, and in that terrible holocaust sweated and strained until at last, at long last, they got control of the great conflagration. Even on the eighteenth day, when success was in sight, the pumps broke down and an alarming situation developed for several hours. A tank collapsed causing a terrific flare-up which led to the explosion of an adjoining tank. Eventually, when the oil became exhausted the flames died down and at last the fire was under control.

Every man who helped to fight that fire was a hero; certain it is that they all shared the tremendous hazards and they all contributed to the splendid combined effort which saved eight oil tanks and possibly a part of the town from destruction. Who, then, decided that certain firemen's services were more valuable than others, that their bravery was greater, that their daring was more glorious? Who decided that George Medals should be awarded to a handful of firemen out of the six hundred? If awards for gallantry had to be made in connection with such an epic battle action - for such it was - the only fair way to have done it would have been to present the chief officer of each brigade engaged with a medal in recognition of the services of his unit. It was no wonder that the deepest dissatisfaction was occasioned locally when the tank fire awards were announced later on. Pembroke, evidently unable to pull the right strings, received no recognition, but a George Medal and a British Empire Medal went to Milford Haven. The indignation of Pembroke and Pembroke Dock people was expressed on all sides and in no uncertain terms, especially with regard to the B.E.M. award to a Milford official who, it was alleged, spent only a short time at the scene of the fire. There was an insistent demand for recognition for Pembroke's Fire Chief, Mr. Arthur Morris, and there is no doubt that if anyone was deserving of a medal it was Mr. Morris who, with his men, was the first on the scene, and did not go to bed for seventeen days. All who were there agreed that he

Full fury ... Another view of the oil tanks blaze at its height.

Roy Hordley

worked without relaxation and regardless of personal risk, setting a splendid example to all. Yet all he received was some minor certificate commending him for his gallantry. Those who attended a special meeting of the Pembroke Borough Council a week after the tanks were bombed will never forget the appearance of Mr. Morris, who took an hour off from his grim task to report to the Council. Beneath the grime which he had not had time to wash off, his pale, drawn face, told eloquently of the ordeal the men were suffering. He was unshaven and his eyes were heavy and red-rimmed. As the meeting progressed it was noticed that on several occasions he almost fell asleep.

Next to the yeoman service of the firemen, perhaps the greatest feature of the historic fire was the magnificent response of the townspeople and members of the Civil Defence Services to the needs of the unprecedented emergency. Wherever one turned men and women of Pembroke Dock were giving their services eagerly - providing accommodation for the firemen, helping feed them, wash them, dress their burns and provide them with a score of needs. There were ample gifts of towels, soap clothes, linen, etc., while some ladies, mostly those of the local Red Cross Detachment and St. John Ambulance Nursing Division, spent hour after hour, day and night, carrying out first-aid work at St. Patrick's Schoolroom. They were described as Angels of Mercy, which, indeed, they were. The following message which the officer in charge of the Bristol contingent asked the *Guardian* to publish at the time provides an indication of how much the local people's efforts were appreciated by the firemen:

"Words are totally inadequate to express the gratitude which the men from Bristol feel towards you. The reception we had and the attentions which have been showered upon us by you wonderful people have really been stupendous. When we left Bristol we knew we were going to a difficult and dangerous task. We expected that we would have to endure all kinds of hardships, that we would have to sleep out 'on the job' in all sorts of conditions and that we would have to exist on the iron rations which we had with us. Instead, we were given the most overwhelming hospitality. Everything was done for us, we were given every comfort and the good ladies even went so far as to bathe our feet. In all our experience we have never known such kindness and we do ask you to accept thanks which come from the very bottom of our hearts".

The five firemen who lost their lives all belonged to the Cardiff Brigade. They were Clifford Mills (31), 118 Brunswick Street, Canton, a son of Mr. Jack Mills, the Welsh Rugby Union referee; Frederick George Davies (31), 6 Llanbradach Street; Ivor John Kilby (29), 44 Gelligaer Street; Trevor Charles Morgan (31), 46 Mey Street, and John Frederick Thomas (30), Elaine Street. These men were working a jet on the tanks just after 1 p.m. on 22nd August, when a large burst of flame enveloped them. Capt. Tom Breakes, Chief Inspector of the Fire Brigades Division of the Home Office, who was standing twenty feet behind the men, stated afterwards that when he last saw them they were trying to retreat. The spurt of flame was caused by a big quantity of oil escaping from the tank where the heat had caused the metal wall to become soft and burst. A memorial service to the five unfortunate men was held in St. Patrick's Church, within a few hundred yards of the blazing inferno, on the following Sunday. There was a large attendance of firemen and of Pembroke Dock people, who felt deeply the loss of the five brave men.

That day, August 22nd, was the most critical of the eighteen days. The death of the five men greatly distressed their colleagues and the spread of raging flames which followed the escape of oil did nothing to re-assure anyone. In fact, there was near-panic for a short time and this spread to the civil population as the fire ran with devilish speed across adjoining

DOCK ATTACKED BY BOMBERS

OIL TANK SET ON FIRE

THREE JUNKERS IN RAID

A dock in South Wales was attacked by enemy bombers on Monday afternoon, and an Air Ministry and Ministry of Home Security communique, stated.

"But the damage was confined to an oil tank, which was set on fire. There were no casualties."

Three Junkers 88 are believed to have taken part in the raid.

Spitfires went up in pursuit and anti-aircraft batteries went into action. An unconfirmed report stated that one 'plane was brought down at sea. No confirmation was possible in the area, though one of the enemy machines was seen by townspeople beating a hasty retreat with smoke pouring from its tail.

The aeroplane dived from the sun and dropped eight bombs. A labourer, who was 100 yards from where the bombs fell, was blown over a fence but was unhurt. Six workmen at the tanks, two watchmen and a cashier who was hand-

rough time. All he wanted was to get away, and get away he did, with the two Spitfires after him. The three of them vanished in the distance, but I am confident that our machines brought that bomber down before he got very far.

FIREMEN MACHINE-GUNNED.

Several firemen are reported to have been injured by machine gun fire. One fireman from Swansea was struck in the ribs by a machine gun bullet, and a number of people are suffering from shock. A Captain of one of the brigades told a "Telegraph" reporter.

"I was engaged as a fireman at a munition works during the last war. Believe me, I saw something then, but it is nothing to compare with what I and others went through this morning.

"We were all fighting the flames for dear life," he went on, "when a Jerry bomber dived from behind

Censor's hand ... How the *Western Telegraph* reported the oil tanks raid. No mention is made of Pembroke Dock - the censor's influence was strong.

countryside, making Military Road impassable and damaging extensively a cottage, farm buildings and crops. In the evening there was another large escape of oil to add to the almost unbelievable difficulties under which the men worked. This produced another wave of alarm amongst the townspeople and started a rumour that another sixty firemen had been burnt to death. So much credence was placed upon this rumour that ambulances rushed to the scene, as well as police, firemen who were off duty and scores of townspeople. Assurances that there had been no further deaths restored public confidence, and the arrival shortly afterwards of re-inforcements from England was a Godsend to the men on the job whose stupendous task was almost beyond endurance.

While the firemen went about their hazardous work in the first hours of the fire they realised acutely that heat and flames and boiling oil were not the only dangers which beset them. They knew that at any moment the enemy might return to try and exact a toll of death from their ranks. It was not a surprise, therefore, when on the Tuesday morning less than twenty-four hours after the blaze had been started a German 'plane dived through the pall of thick black smoke and dropped four bombs. It was a pretty poor effort, however, the bombs exploding half a mile away. A few minutes later the 'plane returned and machine gunned the firemen. There was a stampede for safety, most of the firemen diving beneath the fire engines. A dozen men crouching beneath one engine saw a large number of holes appear in a piece of zinc lying a few feet from them. The zinc had been completely riddled with machine-gun bullets! One fireman was taken to hospital with an injury which was not serious.

Although the fire made an ideal target - it could be seen as far away as the Devonshire coast - the Germans made no attempt to carry out a serious night attack while it burned. On the night of Saturday, August 24th, bombs were dropped and caused damage to hose lines and appliances. There were also some minor casualties but no serious interruption of operations. On Wednesday, the third day of the fire, an enemy machine approached Pembroke Dock from the south-west but three Spitfires went up to intercept and it was driven off. Again, two days later the enemy was in the vicinity but due to our fighter interception no raid developed. There were air raids on the town on September 1st and 2nd but no attempt was made to bomb the tanks.

Statistics do not usually make exciting reading but the following figures regarding this epic blaze are of interest. Of the seventeen tanks at Llanreath, holding approximately 45,000,000 gallons of oil, eleven were destroyed, representing a loss of 33,000,000 gallons. The twenty-two brigades in attendance used 600 men, 53 pumps, nine miles of hose and 2,000 gallons of water per minute. Feeding the men during the eighteen days cost £840. Apart from the five fatal casualties, the numbers receiving treatment were as follows:- Serious cases treated in hospital, 38; minor cases (mostly eyes), 241; burns to the hands, face and neck, 180; sprains and strains, 12; septic feet, 2; foot treatment (due to oil entering boots), 560; cuts and abrasions, 22: gastric cases, 13 - a total of 1,153.

ENEMY AGENTS IN PEMBROKE?

On the afternoon of Sunday, August 25th, when the great Pennar fire had been burning for six days, a German 'plane flew over and dropped two bombs in the vicinity. It was a bold attack, evidently aimed at producing confusion and adding difficulty to the firemen's great task, but again the enemy's bad marksmanship proved a blessing. Both bombs fell near the tanks but caused no military damage although a few firemen received injuries and had to be treated at the Meyrick Hospital. The first bomb fell near a gate at the top of Military Road and uprooted a telegraph pole which flew through the air and, by a freak, landed point downwards a few yards away where it resumed its upright position. The other bomb exploded harmlessly in an open space. Ground defences opened up spiritedly and after unloading its cargo the intruder made hastily out to sea. People who were in Dimond Street as the 'plane flew over witnessed a very unusual occurrence. An army officer was walking down the street and as the bombs whistled down he stopped, unslung a rifle he was carrying over his shoulder, loaded it and took a shot at the 'plane. What he expected to gain by this action is difficult to imagine unless he had hopes of a lucky shot striking a vital part of the aircraft and bringing it down. If he expected to gain the plaudits of the onlookers for a brave act of defiance he was disappointed, for the majority were openly critical of his "sniping" and moved away quickly in case the

Secret snap ... This dramatic photograph, also used as part of the cover illustration, was taken from Hobbs Point, Pembroke Dock, by Roy Hordley, a local soldier home on leave. To take such a picture in wartime one risked a heavy fine or a period of imprisonment, or both. The fact that such a risk was taken many times over means that a photographic record exists of a very trying period in Pembrokeshire's history.

Roy Hordley

raider flew round to seek revenge for the lone rifle shot, which in the excitement of the moment they thought to be a distinct possibility!

The tanks fire gave rise to the first suspicions that spies were lurking in South Pembrokeshire. Inevitably there were many wild and exaggerated stories of suspicious characters flashing lights, secret transmitting sets, raids and arrests by the police, mysterious midnight movements and so on. Ninety per cent of such assertions can safely be written down as being pure assumption produced by the general uneasiness of the times; the remaining ten per cent might have had some foundation in fact. There is every reason to believe, for instance, that enemy agencies were at work during the time of the tanks fire. One night when the blaze was at its height a big car coming from the direction of the tanks pulled up beside half-a-dozen local residents who were talking at the bottom of Military Road. A man, a complete stranger, put his head out of the window and said "Isn't it terrible, twenty men have been burnt to death up there". Then he drove away, never to be seen by any of that half-dozen people again. His story was entirely without foundation. It could not have been due to confusion with the incident in which the five Cardiff firemen lost their lives for it was before that occurrence. Of course, it might have been due to a misunderstanding or a mishearing or it might have been one of those stories which start mysteriously but quite innocently upon such occasions. But those who saw the man in the car were unanimous that there was something suspicious about him. In any event the story he told was one well calculated to produce distress and weakened morale. It was well in keeping with the Goebbels formula later to become so well-known.

One spy story which gained much credence a few weeks later concerned lights which some people vowed they had seen flashing a few miles south of Pembroke on nights when enemy aircraft were in the vicinity. Indeed there were people who began to see lights everywhere, even in Freshwater East, a haven of safety for scores of Pembroke Dock folk. On one memorable night towards the end of the year a few privileged people at The Grotto, that cosy Freshwater rendezvous, where so many from Pembroke Dock were wont to spend their evenings, were let into the secret that two or three Army officers were going out into the darkness to settle once and for all the matter of the lights said to be winking skywards at the bottom of the village. To add drama to the occasion one officer showed his loaded revolver round before buttoning up his trench coat and venturing forth. It was rather in the nature of an anti-climax when they returned to their expectant friends with nothing to report. They had not seen a soul and the black-out was perfect everywhere!

Pembrokeshire people and those in the south of the county in particular were getting precious little rest at nights at this period. Nearly every night the sirens would sound and even if no attack developed the drone of aircraft almost invariably followed which, though it might be in the distance, was sufficient to keep people on the qui vive. And when the sirens were silent sleep was still an uneasy thing, in Pembroke Dock at least, where it had been learnt by grim experience that it was upon such occasions that real attacks

Sky mark ... The oil tanks fire sent smoke billowing hundreds of feet into the air, to be seen as far away as north Devon. This photograph was taken from the main road between Neyland and Honeyborough.

Roy Hordley

occurred. Then there were the 'planes which flew round and round sometimes for an hour and more on end, without any object apparent to the uneasy folk below, unless it was to keep them awake. More often than not, the siren not having sounded, no one knew whether the 'plane was friendly or hostile, and people used to stand on their doorsteps hoping for the best and staring up into the sky watching the long, pointing fingers of the searchlights as they "passed the sound" from one to the other. Upon one such occasion a plane flew back and fore over Pembroke Dock quite unmolested for surely an hour. Then someone's patience must have snapped because an anti-aircraft gun went off with a great bang - and the 'plane was not heard again. These, presumably, were the nuisance raiders. They undoubtedly served a purpose.

People's nerves were beginning to get ragged, as was evidenced by the demand made towards the end of August for the removal of the flag flying over Pembroke Castle which, it was contended, might help enemy 'planes to locate Pembroke Dock! Looking back, the absurdity of the request is apparent. While the castle itself, the harbour and a dozen other aids to navigation remained the flag itself was of no consequence as a guide to the enemy. It is probable that not one enemy airman ever noticed it.

During August a number of bombs were dropped on open spaces and caused no harm. Several fell in the marshland and at Caswell, outside Tenby, on August 17th, while on the last day of the month Morvil Mountain, near Maenclochog, in North Pembrokeshire, was a target. Three of these bombs straddled the Fishguard-Maenclochog road about four miles from the village.

A NIGHT OF AMAZING ESCAPES

Pembroke Dock's lucky star must have been well in the ascendant on Monday, September 2nd, 1940. In the early hours of that morning a raider roared in from the east and, with utter indiscrimination, unloaded a cargo of incendiary and high explosive bombs which completely demolished a number of houses, extensively damaged scores of others, wreaked havoc along the main thoroughfares, scored a direct hit on the Temperance Hall - but did not kill a soul! It was the enemy's second visit that night and the majority of Pembroke Dock people had fallen into uneasy sleep when, some time after I o'clock, without any warning siren, the low flying 'plane awakened them. Almost immediately the bombs crashed down. In Gwyther Street people were scrambling out of bed and running for shelter downstairs when a breathstopping, air-splitting explosion threw them against walls, on to floors, downstairs and, in some cases, out of beds, as their houses heaved and tottered. One bomb had scored a direct hit on the wing at the back of No. 23, Lower Gwyther Street, and another had dropped on No. 32 on the opposite side of the road. No. 32 was completely demolished while the houses each side of it, Nos. 30 and 34, were reduced to shambles, as also was No. 23 on the other side. By remarkable good fortune three of these four houses were empty and the fourth was occupied by only two people who had reached shelter beneath the staircase and escaped unscathed.

No. 32 was the residence of Mr. and Mrs. Young, who had left on the

Blitzed ... Nos. 30 and 32, Gwyther Street, Pembroke Dock, after the raid of September 2nd, 1940. The all but demolished No. 32 was the home of local Stationmaster Mr. W. J. J. Phillips and his family. The houses on each side, Nos. 30 and 34, were reduced to a shambles but, remarkably, no one was killed.

Roy Hordley

previous Saturday for a holiday by the sea. Had they been at home they could not have escaped death or serious injury. The house next door above, No. 34, was the home of Mr. Roch, a lighthousekeeper, his wife and two children. Mr. Roch was away on duty while his wife and children were staying with friends in another district. The house below, No. 30, was occupied by Mr. W. J. J. Phillips, the Pembroke Dock stationmaster, and a former member of the Pembroke Town Council. Mr. Phillips, a Special Constable, was out on duty, but Mrs. Phillips and their daughter were in the house, and when they heard the 'plane they rushed down and under the stairs in their nightclothes - just in the nick of time. No. 23, on the other side, was the home of Mr. Wyrriot Owen, who with his family was staying out of the town.

Neighbours rushed out and stumbling through debris and blinding dust reached the wrecked houses where they immediately commenced rescue work. Mrs. and Miss Phillips were soon located and with little difficulty were brought to safety. White with dust from head to foot, they were taken to Mr. and Mrs. Hordley's house opposite where they soon recovered from their unnerving experience. Later they were joined by friends in the street who, satisfied there was nothing more they could do until morning, spent the remaining hours of darkness singing popular songs with Mr. Fred Hordley, home on leave from the Army, at the piano. Had not the three houses been empty there would almost certainly have been a death roll, which would have added dismay, confusion and difficulty to the havoc of the attack. Yet there were people who continued to campaign bitterly against those who sought safety outside the town.

While the town was still rocking to the explosion of the Gwyther Street bombs, more H.E.'s were falling in the Lewis Street area. One exploded alongside No. 8 Lewis Street, another at the rear of the Bird-in-Hand and another scored a direct hit on the Temperance Hall. The raider's machine guns were blazing but, miraculously no one was hit. Hundreds of small marks noticed next day on the Lewis Street wall of the Temperance Hall were thought to be caused by machine-gun bullets. In the Temperance Hall a number of firemen engaged on the tanks fire were sleeping and eighteen of them received injuries. Two were seriously injured. Fortunately the bomb which struck the hall was a small one and the four main walls of the building withstood the blast. All the same, it was nothing but sheer luck that prevented a heavy death roll. On the other side of the road. the Bird-in-Hand and the houses below it were practically wrecked. Alderman Joe Gibby, landlord of the inn, was trapped by falling masonry, etc., and it was some time before he was released. However, he suffered nothing more than an injury to the foot from which he recovered within a few days. Police and A.R.P. rescue workers performed excellent service that night, especially at the Temperance Hall where the casualties received quick and efficient attention. It was reliably reported that the only mishap occurred when a well-known doctor engaged in giving injections to the wounded had a hypodermic needle accidentally (?) driven into a tender part of his anatomy by a layman assistant standing behind him!

A number of bombs had been dropped previously, a direct hit being scored upon Mrs. Lemon's house on the left hand side going up Tremeyrick Street. Mrs. Lemon, a middle-aged lady, was in the house and when she heard the bomb coming dived under the table for shelter. The house collapsed around her with a sickening crash and she was trapped beneath the debris. Rescue workers were quickly on the scene and after a long and difficult task, made all the worse by the uncertainty as to whether Mrs. Lemon was alive or not, the lady was brought to safety. She was injured and badly shaken but could hardly believe her luck in being alive when she saw the ruins of her home which had been levelled to the ground.

The incendiary bombs used were of the oil type but they did little damage. One fell in the park and another on the corner of Argyle Street - Bush Street, where for months afterwards the walls were covered with black, smelly oil.

The enemy had been busy in the Tenby area earlier that night. Approximately a hundred incendiary bombs were dropped on Kingsmoor Common - miles away from any military objective. Hayricks were set on fire at Enox Hill Farm, Saundersfoot, and Little Kilowen, while between thirty and forty incendiaries were dropped near Netherwood House, Saundersfoot. The Narberth Fire Brigade was soon in action and the fires were extinguished.

Three nights later "Jerry" came again but the attack, from a military point of view, was as abortive as the previous one. Several bombs, high explosive

Devastation ... Another graphic picture of Lower Gwyther Street on the morning of September 2nd, 1940. Before the Luftwaffe's attentions these had been neat terraced houses and gardens of Nos. 30 and 32.

Roy Hordley

and oil type incendiaries, fell in the Castle Hall area, near Milford Haven, apparently an attempt to hit the R.N. Mines Depot. A number of cottages along the Waterston Road were very badly damaged but the occupants escaped without injury. A short time afterwards a 'plane flew over Pembroke Dock and dropped a number of bombs which fell in a field on Bierspool Farm, killing three cows and injuring nine others, the property of Mr. Edward Gibby. Some of the bombs fell quite near to Bierspool House, but did little damage. Mr. and Mrs. Gibby were away from home for the night. Another bomb exploded on the other side of the road near Llanion School and smashed all the windows, while another did similar damage to a number of Llanion houses. Throughout that night raiders roamed the Pembrokeshire sky. The siren sounded twice and it was not until nearly 4.30 that the last all clear sent people thankfully to bed. They were blissfully unaware that before dawn two more "yellow" messages and one "purple" were received at County A.R.P. headquarters at Haverfordwest.

BOMBS ON THE COUNTY TOWN

Haverfordwest had its first taste of bombing on the evening of Tuesday, September 24th - and suddenly realised what Pembroke Dock had been going through! It was just gone 8 o'clock and getting dusk when the 'plane was heard. It was flying quite low and a number of people watched it without any particular concern. Then suddenly it swooped and dropped two bombs. They fell in City Road, one alongside No. 22, Scolton Villas, the home of Miss Sybil Price, the County Dairy Instructress, and the other in Mr. Basil Jones' field about two hundred yards away. The bomb which exploded by Miss Price's house was of heavy calibre and, making a crater fifty feet across and about twenty feet deep, completely demolished the house, extensively damaged about half-a-dozen others in the row and some opposite, including the shop and sub-Post Office. Up and down the street windows were smashed and slates ripped from roofs. Again, by an act of providence, no one was killed. Miss Price had left her house two minutes before to accompany on their way home some friends who had been visiting her. She had pressed her friends to stay but they wanted to get home.

Luck was also with Mr. Walter Hardacre whose front door faced the crater and was only a couple of yards from its lip. He was in the garden at the rear of the house and was flung some way by the blast, but escaped with cuts and bruises. His wife, who was in the house, was shocked and slightly cut when all the windows blew in. Another casualty was 14-year-old Willie Lewis, living at 62, City Road, on the opposite side of the road. He was going into his house when the bombs whistled down. A big chunk of masonry came whizzing through the air and caught him on the left thigh. Shocked and rather badly injured, he had to be removed to hospital. People living in the vicinity had some remarkable escapes as stones and debris came crashing through their roofs and windows and glass flew everywhere. Others walking along the street were equally lucky. Viewing the havoc the following morning a City Road resident remarked "The age of miracles has not passed - just imagine, all this and no one killed!" A miracle it was indeed.

Bombs also fell in the New Road area, causing extensive damage to houses there, but no personal injuries.

The explosions rocked the whole town. Coming so suddenly and unexpectedly - again there was no warning siren - the town was greatly shocked but recovered itself admirably within minutes. Demolition squads and A.R.P. and A.F.S. units were on the scene with commendable promptitude and set to work with a will. Large audiences at the two cinemas had some bad moments as they felt the buildings tremble, but the shows went on and there was no panic. Local Scouts were holding a meeting at the Wesleyan Schoolroom and Mr. Harold Thomas, their scoutmaster, immediately put them to sing, which proved an excellent way of restoring the youthful nerve. Windows in the chapel had been smashed by the blast. Meanwhile, people in Pembroke Dock, seeing the flash in the darkening sky

County town ... Haverfordwest became a target on September 24th, 1940, when bombs fell in City Road and New Road. This aeriel view was taken from a Sunderland flying boat later in the war.

John Evans Collection

to the north followed by the dull thud of the explosion, looked at each other in wonderment and said, "It looks as if Harfat is copping it this time!" It is thought that this raider was being pursued by Spitfires and jettisoned its bombs to gain speed, anything making a target, even a row of inoffensive Council houses. People on the St. Davids Road spoke of seeing another 'plane, while Mrs. J. Fortune, returning from Newgale on her bicycle, said that spent machine-gun bullets fell in the road around her.

Incidents had occurred several nights previously. Just after midnight on September 7th, two bombs fell at West Pennar while on September 11th one dropped two hundred yards from Templeton School but failed to explode Another two unexploded bombs fell at the Observatory Field, Hakin, and near Milton Farm, Burton, on the following night, while incendiaries were dropped in the Rhoscrowther district.

The Luftwaffe was also making repeated attacks on our shipping and Milford trawlers were getting a rough time. The first Milford fisherman victim of Nazi air attack was Second Engineer Tom Aldsworth Lamb, a 25 year-old single man from Croesgoch. His trawler was fishing to the southwest when it was attacked by a Heinkel. Mr. Lamb was talking to the skipper, Mr. J. Scoble, when machine-gun bullets ripped through the wheelhouse where they were standing. The skipper had fallen flat and escaped. Mr. Lamb, down on one knee, was hit in the head and killed instantly. About the same time another Milford boat, skippered by Mr. J. Utting, was attacked by three German 'planes. Twelve bombs were dropped but thanks to clever manoeuvring they all missed the boat. Within the next few days, three Milford Haven trawlers were lost. One, the *"John Baptist"*, belonging to Milford Fisheries and skippered by Mr. W. J. McLean, was lost without trace, and it was presumed that the vessel and the twelve members of its crew perished in an air attack. The second trawler, the "*Bass Rock*", belonging to Mr. W. H. East, was bombed and sunk, the skipper, Mr. Alfred Skewis, and three members of the crew losing their lives. The attack was made by a Dornier which dived out of the sun with its engines shut off. Hit twice, the trawler began to sink and as the survivors were trying to launch the lifeboat the Germans came back to machine-gun them. Two of Messrs. Yolland and Llewellin's trawlers were in the vicinity and gave the 'plane a hot reception. Skipper Arthur Howie, on one of them, ordered his crew to take shelter, manned the defensive gun himself and fired 160 rounds at the attacker scoring, it was believed, several hits. These two trawlers picked up five survivors of the ill-fated vessel and brought them into Milford Haven. The third vessel left for the fishing grounds on Wednesday, September 11th, and did not return. It was the *Respondo*, owned by Messrs. Yolland and Llewellin and the skipper was Mr. T. R. Owston, Priory Road, Milford Haven. This loss brought the number of missing in the three disasters up to twenty-eight.

Pembroke Borough continued to call out for adequate air raid shelters. While the shelters being erected for the schools were described as the best in Wales there was the utmost dissatisfaction at the County Council's communal shelters. It was stated in responsible quarters that they could be knocked over with a seven-pound hammer and spirited protests were made to the appropriate quarters. A little later, because of the continued failure of the official air raid warning system, many streets in Pembroke Dock devised a scheme of their own. The men in these streets, or the majority of them at least, took it in turn to stay up nights and at the first sign of a possible attack give warning to their neighbours who were thus enabled to sleep with easier minds. Generally speaking, this scheme worked very well but inevitably there were those who, for reasons best known to themselves, declined to take part.

CHARMED VILLAGE

Of all the military objectives in Pembrokeshire - and there were quite a few - probably Milton aerodrome took most punishment from German bombs, apart of course from the oil tanks. The Hun airmen appeared to have no difficulty in locating the airfield, a fact the sensationalists were wont to ascribe to a super German spy system but which was more probably due to the site being an old one which was used for a period at the end of the First World War. Whatever the reason, "Jerry" came on a number of occasions to unload a deadly cargo upon the runways and hangars of the aerodrome always referred to in the R.A.F. as Carew Cheriton. One of the worst attacks to rock this pretty, wooded corner of rural Pembrokeshire occurred just before 7 a.m. on Tuesday, October 1st, 1940. It was a dull morning and the 'planes, one bomber and two fighters, approached under cloud cover and then dived on the aerodrome, releasing a salvo of bombs and at the same time opening up with machine guns. The bombs, high explosive and incendiary, fell across the aerodrome, causing fires in the hangars, disrupting communications and damaging 'planes. One airman was killed and six seriously injured. Four others were slightly injured. Fortunately, several of the bombs failed to explode. Some incendiaries fell in Carew village, while one high explosive landed in the main road near the old entrance to the aerodrome. Altogether the raid was quite an effective one from the enemy's viewpoint, but once again the number of casualties was miraculously low.

Camouflage ... Despite the efforts of the camouflage experts the RAF airfield at Carew Cheriton remained a prominent feature on the county landscape, and was raided a number of times. This view was taken from a Blenheim from 3,000 feet on May 7th, 1942.

Dick Lindley

37

The Luftwaffe had been busy over Pembrokeshire all that night, but apart from this raid at Milton their efforts were pretty scrabbly. Mostly incendiaries were used and they were dropped at widely scattered points with no apparent plan. Many of these fire bombs burnt themselves out harmlessly in the Herbrandston locality, others fell in the Cuffern, Roch and Hayscastle areas, but the only casualties were some cattle and sheep. Two high explosives whistled to earth alongside Start Farm on Cuffern Mountain, but failed to go off. The farm residents were so little perturbed that not only did they decline to get out of bed but next day insisted on carrying on their work around the house as usual despite the dynamite buried a few yards away. Was there ever such sang froid!

These roaming, indefinite air attacks had gone on throughout the previous week. On September 27th a lone raider dropped a few incendiaries around the Neyland area - three on the beach, two on the promenade, three in the nearby fields and others at Scoveston and Waterston. The next night he came again to unload some incendiaries near Steynton, which caused neither damage nor casualties. There was also a strange "attack" upon Haverfordwest. A 'plane flying in from the west and passing to the north of the town dropped ten bombs which exploded harmlessly in a bunch in a field near Tangiers. The bombs were very small ones and were thought to have been released in a container. For some hours mystery surrounded this incident because no one could find the place where the bombs exploded. It was broad daylight the next day, Sunday, when the craters were discovered, far from house or habitation and miles from any military objective - a typical piece of "strategy" by the much vaunted Luftwaffe.

On the same night the coastguard at Linney Head extinguished an unusual type of bomb. It was of the incendiary type but was round and about the size of a ball. Two nights later incendiaries were dropped at points as far apart as Trecwn and Rosepool, Little Haven. High explosives fell between Hayscastle and Plumstone Mountain, but again it was a futile night for "Jerry". He achieved nothing militarily and precious little in any other way.

For sheer senselessness and brutality, however, the bombing of Tiers Cross village, near Haverfordwest, on the night of October 5th was the classic of the Pembrokeshire raids. But the village was charmed, taking the full impact of eight high explosive bombs and a number of incendiaries without a fatal casualty. Flying so low that lights could be seen in the cabin windows the 'plane skimmed the chimney pots of the County Town going in a south-westerly direction. It was making a loud and unusual noise and many people watching it in the gathering dusk thought it was going to crash. At Merlin's Bridge it released a number of incendiaries which fell alongside the railway line and then at Tiers Cross the high explosives crashed down right across the small village, less than fifty yards separating one from the other. Although it was growing dark the pilot could not have failed to see the little cluster of houses as he was barely clearing the trees as he approached. Every house in the village received some sort of damage and some were completely demolished but only two people were taken to hospital - Mr. Harry

Thomas and his son, Mr. Charles Thomas, whose cottage collapsed about them. Fortunately the bombs were not very large ones - they were thought to be 125 pounders - but all the same it was nothing short of a miracle that half the residents were not killed or seriously injured. The next day was Sunday and large congregations attended at Tiers Cross Congregational Church to offer prayers of thankfulness. Only one pane in the chapel was damaged although all the windows in the adjoining schoolroom were smashed.

With so much indiscriminate bombing going on the people had reached the stage where they regarded no place as immune, the general attitude being well exemplified by a serious suggestion at a meeting of Pembroke R.D.C. that Jameston Council houses looked like a hospital from the air and would therefore be an outstanding target for the enemy!

'UNOFFICIAL' RAIDS

Discontent at the arrangements for sounding the siren reached a critical pitch in Pembroke Dock following two raids which occurred without warning, within an hour of each other on the night of Wednesday, October 16th. The first raid was shortly before 9 o'clock. It was made by a single 'plane which after dropping a number of flares released a string of high explosive and incendiary bombs. Some people in the streets had seen the flares and were prepared for trouble but to the majority the sickening crash of the bombs, now all too familiar, was the first intimation that "'Jerry' was over again". A devil's chorus of explosions and machine gun fire continued for several minutes and then there was silence. After half-an-hour or so the more venturesome left their shelter, persuaded by the quietness which then reigned, that it was all clear. But within ten minutes the raider was back and caught scores of people in the streets as he released another load of bombs.

Again there was hurrying into shelters and in the absence of anything to assure them that the danger was over many people remained in refuge, cold, shivering and apprehensive, for hours, some until the first streaks of dawn had shot across the sky. The next morning irate citizens went to the A.R.P. report centre to know why no siren had been sounded, firstly to give warning of the raid and secondly to show that the raid was over. They were told that officially there had been no raid, an answer which provoked some interesting comment as the enquirers made their way home through the glass strewn streets. If this was an unofficial raid what, asked one, would an official raid be like? Other suggestions were that the siren should be taken down and presented to the nation as disused iron and that other uses should be made of the materials which went to build the public shelters as the doors of these much maligned little structures were found to be padlocked when people ran to them during the second attack. Another suggestion, and one that was made quite seriously, was that the County A.R.P. headquarters should move from Haverfordwest to Pembroke Dock which was obviously the centre of attraction to the Germans. It was thought that the town's grievances would then have some attention!

So great was the public discontent that the Borough Council decided to communicate with the Prime Minister, the Minister of Home Security, the War Office and the Regional A.R.P. Commissioner on the matter. A public protest meeting in Pembroke Dock was also arranged but it had to be abandoned because no suitable building with an adequate black-out was available. While there is no doubt that Pembroke Dock had every reason for its concern, in retrospect it is obvious that a system permitting warnings at local discretion, which was much in demand, would not have been a satisfactory solution of the problem. On the contrary it is possible that such a system would only have produced greater confusion and added to the perils of the people. There was a general tendency to blame the County A.R.P. system for all the troubles, but the fact was that the County officials were quite powerless, being entirely under the control of Cardiff. In turn, Cardiff

New airfield ... The German air force were well aware of the new airfield being established at Angle, long before it became operational. This Luftwaffe photograph, dated May, 1941, has been marked to show the extent of the new airfield and the alignment of its runways.

Via Roy Belcher

was dependent upon Fighter Command who should have been in a better position than anyone in Pembroke Dock to know the movement of enemy planes over the country. That Fighter Command "fell down on the job" on so many occasions in the early days was doubtless due to the fact that the system had not by then adjusted itself to the unexpected conditions caused by the French surrender.

Between twenty and thirty H.E. bombs, some of them of the delayed action type, and several incendiaries fell at widespread points that Wednesday night. Several long bursts of machine-gun fire featured the attack and it is thought that on one occasion at least, the raider was firing into the streets. But it was another night of good fortune: no one was killed, only one man was slightly injured, no damage of military importance was done and damage to civilian property was comparatively slight. The explosive bombs landed in King Street Lane, Wellington Street, Milton Terrace and the top of the town, one in the cemetery in Upper Park Street and another (delayed action type) in Hawkestone Road. The Bomb Disposal Squad set to work on the time bomb without delay and the following day it was driven away on a lorry before a little crowd of spectators, very interested and still just a little apprehensive!

If the raider had dropped a bomb on Albion Square during its second visit, Pembroke Dock would have lost several distinguished inhabitants. Quite a crowd of people, including a few members of the Town Council who had been inspecting the damage caused by the bomb which fell at the top of Wellington Street half-an-hour before, were gathered about the square when the 'plane returned. Indeed, all over the town people were standing on the pavement talking about the raid and, it can safely be surmised, making caustic comments about the siren arrangements. Then came the roar of aero engines again and there was a stampede for shelter into doorways and gutters, under walls and out into the open. On the strength of the fallacious theory that a bomb never drops in the same place twice, a number of people, including the author and at least one member of the Borough Council, Alderman J. R. Williams, jumped into the crater at the top of Wellington Street and there lay face downwards as hell broke loose around. As the bombs whistled somebody shouted a warning and girls crouching in the doorways down Wellington Street began to scream. The 'plane, big and black against the moonlit sky came tearing low overhead, its machine-guns blazing. At the same time a lively defence was put up by the guns in the Air Station, the tracers streaking up and down the sky, creating a pattern at once beautiful and terrifying. Then the raider was gone and all was quiet again.

Another attack on Pembroke Dock occurred on the following Sunday night. Only incendiaries were dropped, and two houses were set on fire, one at the corner of Bush Street and Gwyther Street and the other in Laws Street. The other incendiaries were quickly and effectively dealt with, some in the streets, others in gardens and fields and one or two on doorsteps. On the same night some explosive bombs fell harmlessly between Monkton and Hundleton and incendiaries at Monkton, West Pennar, Hakin and Hayscastle, all without any serious effect. On the previous Sunday six high explosives were dropped at Milton Aerodrome, damaging one hangar, the N.A.A.F.I. buildings and some huts. A Dutch officer received some injuries.

FIRST CIVILIAN CASUALTIES

Pembroke Dock's almost phenomenal run of luck in sustaining repeated air attacks without any fatal civilian casualties came to an end on November 6th 1940. Shortly after 6 o'clock that morning a number of 'planes raided the town and killed three civilians and one Serviceman. The victims were Mr. and Mrs. W. Kinton who carried on an old established grocery business in Bush Street, Mrs. Harvey, whose husband, Dr. Harvey, had only just taken over the practice of the late Dr. Rufus Rees and who lived next door; and a young R.A.F. man who was lodging with Mr. and Mrs. Kinton. Dr. Harvey was seriously injured but their small baby had a miraculous escape The trail of death left by the raid created a profound impression throughout the Borough. Mr. and Mrs. Kinton were well known inhabitants of advanced years whose old-world charm and kindliness had endeared them to scores of friends. It was indeed a cruel twist of fate that the violence of war should end two such serene and peaceful lives.

The chill and darkness of a November morning had not begun to dissolve when the siren wailed its mournful warning. Almost at once the drone of aeroplanes filled the air. It was a peculiar sound; the note of the engines seemed different from that heard on previous occasions and later there was considerable speculation as to what type of aircraft was used, some

Spitfire ... The major German raids on Pembrokeshire were all but over by the time the fighter station, RAF Angle, became operational. Various squadrons, mainly with Hurricanes and Spitfires, were stationed here in 1942 and 1943. Here a Spitfire Vb of No. 312 (Czech) Squadron, RAF, is seen against a backdrop of the cliff edge and the sea. The pilot was Sergeant (later Squadron Leader) Tony Liskutin, who had escaped from his native Czechoslovakia to continue the fight from Britain.

Squadron Leader M. A. Liskutin

43

suggesting that they were Italian machines. Whatever they were, there were several of them, and they carried out a violent and indiscriminate attack. It is estimated that nearly thirty high explosives were dropped and most of them were of heavy calibre, causing huge craters. Eight of these bombs fell in the County School playing field, three in the Memorial Park and one (unexploded) near the Llanion tanks. Others dropped in Bush Street, scoring a direct hit on Mr. and Mrs. Kinton's house, in the Co-op. Lane, Prince's Street, Dockyard Avenue and alongside the Military Hospital, where there were some casualties and considerable damage.

Mr. and Mrs. Kinton's house was completely demolished, burying them beneath the stairs where apparently they were sleeping. Demolition and rescue workers rushed to the scene and worked feverishly for over two hours to extricate the unfortunate people. It was hoped that Mrs. Kinton would be saved as she was heard to speak when the rescue work was in progress, but when extricated it was found she had passed away. By this time a large crowd had gathered and the people watched silently and with bowed heads as the bodies of Mr. and Mrs. Kinton were carried away to the mortuary. The body of the young Air Force man, in night clothing, was found on the pavement outside the premises. He was beyond human aid. Another lodger, Mr. T. H. Clement, a clerk in the Pembroke Dock branch of Barclays Bank, escaped with serious injuries and was taken to the Meyrick Hospital.

Heroic work by rescuers failed to save Mrs. Harvey next door, where a fire was burning, due, it is thought, to the domestic fire in the house spreading when the house collapsed. Dr. Harvey was extricated badly injured and was removed to hospital, while the baby escaped unscathed due to the presence of mind of Mrs. Harvey, who although partly buried by the debris, and on the point of collapse, threw the child clear of the fire into the passage. There it was found uninjured hanging by its clothing to a clothes peg on the wall! Bush Street from the junction of Park Street to Albion Square, was a veritable shambles. All the shops and houses around were extensively damaged, windows being shattered, doors blown in and roofs crushed by falling stones. People living in the locality had wonderful escapes, many being unhurt although parts of their houses fell in on them.

The bravery of A.R.P., fire-fighting and police personnel in the Bush Street rescue efforts won the commendation of everyone and two police officers, Sergt. Bodman and P.C. Humphreys, subsequently received decorations for their outstanding work.

On the following Sunday night, November 10th, when the enemy made his next visit, a local Civil Defence worker, exasperated at what he considered to be red tape obstructing common-sense procedure, put the siren off without permission - and got into hot water with the authorities. But he was on perfectly safe ground. The voice of the people rose up in his defence and he was acclaimed a hero. His unauthorised action undoubtedly saved several people from injury or death and had the threats of dire punishment, including imprisonment, been carried out there would most assuredly have been a public revolt on an unprecedented scale. The central figure of this interesting incident was Alderman J. R. Williams, one of the most vociferous advocates of reform of the siren system. At that time Alderman Williams, the vice-chairman of the old Fire Brigade Committee of the Borough Council, slept most nights at the Fire Station at the Market Hall. He was there on Sunday night and when, about midnight, the familiar discordant note of enemy 'planes was heard, he ordered a fireman, Mr. Harry Baker, to press the button. A few minutes later bombs crashed down on houses which had just been vacated by persons who had run for shelter upon hearing the warning. It is understood that Alderman Williams subsequently received some serious letters on the matter, but he remained unperturbed and with everyone stoutly defending his action, nothing came of it.

All the bombs in that Sunday night raid fell in the top part of Pembroke Dock. A direct hit was scored on 19, Owen Street, Pennar, but the occupants, Mr. and Mrs. Scourfield, were sheltering beneath the stairs, and had a wonderful escape. On Bethany corner three bombs fell together, the points of impact forming an isosceles triangle. One of these bombs completely destroyed an empty fish and chip shop next door to the Caledonia public house and tore away part of the inn. The landlord, Mr. Beynon, with his wife and members of the family were sitting in their kitchen and were unhurt. Undeterred by the extensive damage to their premises and the loss of a lot of stock, the Beynons opened again for business without loss of time, an action much appreciated by the many local patrons of this old established house. The second bomb struck No. 11, just opposite the chip shop, the residence of Mrs. Emment, who, fortunately, had run for shelter to the cellar of a neighbour's house nearby upon hearing the siren. Mrs. Griffiths next door and Mr. Joe Davies and members of his family from next door to the chip shop had also gone to the neighbour's cellar and thus escaped. "Thank God for the siren", was the fervent expressions of these people the next day. The third bomb fell on Bethany Baptist Chapel and caused considerable damage.

Members of the Pembrokeshire Constabulary had narrow escapes. The Police patrol car had only just passed Bethany and was going up High Street when the bombs dropped. It "bounced" with the explosion and it can be safely assumed that the speed cop then put on a bit more speed! A constable on foot, P.C. Greenslade (later Sergt. Greenslade,) was standing in the narrow street running up alongside the chapel when he heard the warning whistle. He lay flat and was uninjured. Other bombs, H.E. and incendiary, fell around Cross Park and Pennar and caused some damage but no casualties.

THE BIG BLITZ

Although no concentrated attack occurred between November 6th, 1940, and May 12th, 1941, the night skies over Pembrokeshire were hardly ever free of the hum of aircraft and the flash and crack of ack-ack fire during that period. It was a period of uneasiness. Night after night the sirens wailed, followed in a few minutes by the sound of aircraft approaching from the south. Hearts beat a little faster as the steady rise and fall of Junkers and Heinkel engines grew louder and louder until at last the sound of them filled the whole of the heavens. Sometimes a bomb or two or a single parachute mine or a bunch of incendiaries would be dropped at random; sometimes the metallic rattle of a machine-gun would provide a sharp contrast of sound against the deep note of the bombers, sometimes a low flying raider would fly round and round as if in an intense search. But no major attack developed. As the weeks of 1941 wore on the bombers became more and more inclined to leave Pembrokeshire alone, flying high over the area in their hundreds to attack Merseyside, the Midlands and Northern Ireland.

This, however, did not ease the minds of the local people who almost every night, at about the same hour, had to leave their beds or their firesides to go to shelter or out on A.R.P. duty. As the hordes came over, the big guns down the harbour would start firing and between the scores of searchlights, ack-ack bursts like splashes of gold dust would add colour to the beautiful lattice pattern in the sky. Sometimes, but not very often, an aircraft would get caught in a searchlight beam and, small and glistening thousands of feet above the earth and looking so pretty and harmless, it would turn and twist while all the guns for miles around opened up. For hours the all-pervading drone of the 'planes with the intermittent crack of the guns and the zip of falling shrapnel would go on until at last the final flight had passed on its mission of death to the north. A lapse of perhaps half-an-hour and the performance would start all over again as the bombers hooked it for home, obviously in less orderly flight and some of them making ominous noises which spoke of rough handling by our ground defences and night-fighters. The next morning the news bulletins would tell which town had received the bombardment. Liverpool and Merseyside were attacked time and again. Swansea had its merciless three nights blitz. Midland towns were bombed. Belfast had its turn and even Dublin, neutral and well lighted, became an objective on one occasion. All these nights Pembrokeshire watched, listened and waited. There was an inescapable feeling that one night it would be Pembroke Dock's turn and, sure enough, it came on May 12th, when the town was almost reduced to a shambles under the terrific bombardment.

The sirens had sounded on sixteen out of the eighteen nights preceding May 12th, sometimes twice within a few hours. It was not out of the scheme of things, therefore, when a "red" message set the banshees wailing again at a minute after midnight on the night of May 11th - 12th. Almost at once the sound of aircraft filled the sky. It was soon apparent that these were not the usual high flyers winging their way northward. They were at comparatively low altitude and wheeling round the area. Everybody waited in grim expectancy. Was this it?

Port of call ... Luftwaffe bombers ranged far and wide over Britain in 1940 and 1941, taking photographs of military targets as well as bombing them. This view of the important port of Fishguard was taken on one such reconnaissance flight. A ferry port linking to the Irish Republic, Fishguard lost one of its ferries - the *St. Patrick* - in June, 1941, when the vessel was bombed and sunk by German aircraft.

Via Studio Jon

Nearly an hour passed without the circling 'planes having given any indication of friendship or hostility. Not a gun had been fired at them. The optimists were cheerfully proclaiming "They're ours" and some had indeed gone back to their warm beds when about I a.m. a sharp whistle ripped the air and the rear of Mr. T. P. Owen's premises in Park Street went up in the air as a bomb exploded with a great crash in his garden.

So began a night of terror, the story of which will be told as long as Pembroke Dock exists. High explosives and incendiaries rained down and, between them came many land mines, their parachutes flapping softly in the light night breeze. It was the first time land mines had been used in a local attack of any scale and they proved a terrifying weapon. While the ordinary bombs whistled down and exploded in a matter of seconds, the land mines rustled down slowly over the town, struck earth with a dull thud and then, after a few moments of ominous silence, went off with a mighty crack, wreaking havoc all around. One of the first of the mines to fall, its long, round container swinging back and fore, was mistaken for a parachutist, whilst another swishing over Park Street was thought by Mr. W. G. Munro, crouching beside his house, to be a 'plane coming down with its engines cut

47

out. It is estimated that fifteen land mines were released over Pembroke Dock that night. A number of them including some that fell in the mud off the bottom of Water Street failed to explode but those that did caused tremendous havoc.

When at last the full cost of the raid was counted up it was found that the town had suffered grievously. The death rate was practically five per thousand, which was much higher than that suffered in one raid in most of the bigger towns. The next day it was found that thirty civilians and two servicemen had been killed, four were missing and a large number injured. Parts of three human bodies could not be identified. Nearly 2,000 houses were damaged. A similar death roll would have given London 40,000 dead in one raid. Glasgow and Birmingham about 5,400, Liverpool 4,280, Cardiff over 1,000 and Swansea over 800.

The raid revealed very vividly the lack of preparation for a raid of such extent. One regrettable feature was the lack of feeding arrangements by the County Council Public Assistance Committee. It is on record that when large numbers gathered at the Wesley Hall to be fed, only one small spirit stove was available to boil water. Later in the day the feeding arrangements were improved with the arrival of the Queen's Mobile Canteens. In this connection, mention must be made of the excellent work of the local W.V.S. mobile canteen which proved a veritable boon in the confused and frightened hours immediately after the raid. Started in the winter of 1940 by the County W.V.S. organisers, Miss N. Thomas, J.P., and Mrs. Salmond, Saundersfoot, this canteen had performed grand service in the lonely military sites along the haven but it was after the big, blitz that its full value

In ruins ... The late Dr. Stewart's house at the junction of Lower Gwyther Street and Apley Terrace, Pembroke Dock, was severely damaged in the May 11th/12th, 1941, blitz. In the background is part of the railway station.

Mrs. D. Waters

48

was felt. A telephone message in the middle of the night to the then Mrs. Burleigh Leach, at the time the W.V.S. Centre Organiser for Castlemartin area, resulted in the prompt arrival of the mobile canteen in Pembroke Dock where it remained until about 4 to 5 p.m. the following afternoon. The canteen, in charge of Mrs. Burleigh Leach and Mrs. Pinchard, operated on its own until about midday when it was joined by other mobile canteens. The total absence of an information bureau was also keenly felt. Many hundreds of people who had suffered in some way or another were at a complete loss to know what to do for sustenance and advice. Had there been a central bureau much confusion would have been avoided. A compensating feature, however, was the wonderful way in which the surrounding areas rallied to the aid of the stricken town. They showed their sympathy in a thousand practical ways, the wonderful help-your-neighbour spirit which has never failed to reveal itself amongst British people in an emergency being a bright and steady beacon in those dark, desperate days.

TOWN OF ECHOES

The heavy raid of May 12th developed according to the familiar Goering formula of incendiaries followed by high explosives. Most of the explosives were of very heavy calibre (for those days) and levelled several buildings completely to the ground. One fell right on the Pier Hotel, burying the proprietor, Mr. Rhys Morris, formerly of Haverfordwest and a native of the Solva district, and a number of people who were staying there. The Criterion Hotel across the road was almost completely demolished while along Pier Road the roofs of all the buildings were blown off and the windows shattered, There was extensive damage in the Ordnance Factory, caused it is believed, by a mine which exploded in the water near Hancock's Yard. Other devastation in this area was at the Gas Works, which received a direct hit. The laundry was destroyed while Squibbs' photography premises on the other side of the road also went up in flames and was burnt out completely.

Meanwhile, a mine had parachuted down behind lower Laws Street and, exploding with a terrific detonation, laid in ruins a number of houses. Several old, respected and loved residents perished beneath the ruins. Amongst the houses destroyed was the Three Crowns, one of the most popular and cosy inns of pre-war Pembroke Dock. But the landlord, Mr. Alf Bowen and his good wife were brought out alive from the beneath the debris the following day. They recovered slowly but life was never the same for them again. Having regard to the devastation in the street and to the Three Crowns itself, it was a remarkable

Hotels no more ... On the night of May 11th/12th, 1941, bombs cut a swathe through houses and hotels at the Tremeyrick Street/Llanion Terrace/Water Street area of Pembroke Dock. This is the view which greeted the battered townspeople for the rest of the war. The Pier Hotel (centre) is no more and the nearby Criterion Hotel was also almost completely demolished.

Roy Hordley

rescue, aided to no small extent by the steadfastness with which Mr. and Mrs. Bowen faced the terrible ordeal.

Another public house, the Prince Albert, also received a direct hit, the landlady, Mrs. Mary Elizabeth Treharne Evans, and several residents being killed. The Market House was extensively damaged as also were the new houses up at Park View Crescent where a mine touched down only ten yards away from the rear of the premises. The residents of these the town's newest properties had a really amazing escape. But they were undaunted, their fine spirit being typified by Mr. P. Castle, who, immediately after the raid, hoisted a Union Jack over his shattered home where it fluttered proudly during the sombre weeks which followed.

It would require a large volume to describe in detail all the scores of incidents of this savage raid. Death and destruction were abroad that night in their fullest fury but providence was there too, for numerous were the hairbreadth escapes and great were the strength and courage which, flowing steadily from a source beyond the control of man, enabled the aged, the weak and the young to bear the ordeal, and the brave to go forth into the holocaust to perform their matchless deeds of rescue. It is certain that the civil defences met the crisis with unflinching steadfastness and performed their work in a manner which left no room for criticism. With so much heroism crammed into so few hours it would be an impossible task to select fairly those deserving of special commendation. Many heroes there were whose work became known and was rightly praised but doubtless many brave deeds will for ever remain untold. It is better, therefore, to refrain from mentioning the names of many gallant people which come readily to mind. Sufficient be it to say that that night they were put to the test and were not found wanting.

The raid interrupted the gas and electricity supplies and for some time the ferry boat was stopped from running owing to the danger of mines in the harbour. For several days afterwards a minesweeper swept the path of the ferry boat before it crossed to and from Neyland.

A ghastly spectacle was presented by the light of Monday's dawn. Buildings lay in ruins, debris inches thick covered most streets and here and there on heaps of rubble rescue workers, pale, drawn and haggard, continued their task with infinite care knowing that at any moment they might find a human body. Everywhere there was devastation and people stood in little knots about the street talking in shocked tones about the events of the night. As the day wore on and the full extent of the tragedy became known residents, sick at heart, attempted to set about their own affairs, striving desperately to reconcile themselves to the terrible loss the town had suffered in life and property. But concentration in such chaos was an impossible thing and sadly people gathered their valuables together and prepared to leave the town for the night.

The Luftwaffe had been making a habit for some weeks to raid the same town on two or three successive nights and Pembroke Dock had not forgotten this fact when, early in the afternoon of May 12th, a great exodus from the town began. There was a real and understandable fear that the raiders would come again that night and thousands sought refuge outside the town, the complaints and criticisms about "fleeing to the mountains", so frequent a week before, being forgotten in the overwhelming crisis of the moment. It was not only the rank and file of the civilian population who feared another attack on the second night. Hundreds of Servicemen billeted locally were given the order "Get out of the town. Sleep where you like, but keep away until tomorrow morning". As dusk gathered military trucks went round the streets and men, women and children piled into them to be carried away from the danger area.

Refugees fleeing along the roads of France a year before could hardly have presented a more pathetic picture than the people of Pembroke Dock as they poured out of the town that bright Spring evening. An unforgettable scene was witnessed at the Mill Bridge, Pembroke. Down over the hill from Pembroke Dock they came in an endless stream, in cars, lorries and overloaded buses, on motorcycles, bicycles and horse-drawn carts and wagons. Hundreds came on foot, weary mothers with infants in arms and little boys and girls hardly of school age running behind, wonderment written plain on their pale faces; old men on sticks, young men with grim expressions, subdued boys and frightened girls. Nearly every person clutched tightly some valued possession. Many of the vehicles were piled high with articles of furniture and household ware. Dogs, cats, caged birds and parrots accompanied their owners. Many of the older folk obviously found it difficult to get along. Women bit their lips and some failed to stem the tears that filled their eyes. Children's noise and chatter and high spirits were nowhere to be found. There was no spark of gaiety, no sign of happiness in that motley, unending procession. Dusk fell and still they came, and long after the stars had studded the sky there were stragglers hurrying from a devastated town.

Where did they go? Hundreds stayed in Pembroke where good people threw open their homes in a grand gesture of neighbourliness, and schools and schoolrooms and vestries were quickly converted into sleeping quarters by many willing hands. Probably the population of Pembroke was doubled for that memorable night and, in fact, for many nights to come. Tenby took in scores and so did Freshwater; many went to Haverfordwest and Neyland while others were given sanctuary in the villages and farmhouses of South Pembrokeshire. But not everybody found shelter. There were those who, with no friends or relatives outside the town and no money with which to pay for a roof over their heads, had to face the night in Pembroke Dock or flee to the open country. It is a fact that many people slept in the open in Bush Woods and the surrounding fields and hedges for nights after May 12th.

Pembroke Dock was a dark, deserted, dismal town that night. No more than a few hundred remained to face whatever the midnight hours held and the few who walked the streets had no company except the echo of their own footsteps through the empty houses. And so it was the next night and for many nights after until gradually with the general slackening of the air attacks, people began to return to their shattered homes.

As was expected the raiders came again in the early hours of May 13th, but no bombs were dropped on Pembroke Dock. The target that night was Milton Aerodrome, several high explosives falling in and around the village, two at Ratford Farm, one on the road outside Milton House and another (unexploded) in the drive.

Scars... The scars of the night-time blitz on May I I th/May 12th, 1941, show on the buildings near Pembroke Dock's Market. This photograph was taken later in the war when personnel from the RAF Station, including members of the Women's Auxiliary Air Force, were on parade.

Via Vernon Scott

RATTLING OF TEN THOUSAND BONES

When the Germans made their next - and last - big raid on Pembroke Dock, on the night of June 11th, 1941, the town was still largely unpopulated and thus a second heavy death roll was avoided. Although several high explosives were used, this was really an incendiary attack. Locally it is still referred to as "the fire blitz" which is an accurate and expressive description of a memorable night. Thousands of incendiaries were showered over the town and fires sprang up at scattered points. As the flames gained hold, high explosives crashed down, hindering the work of the fire fighters who turned out very quickly and performed valued service.

Several 'planes took part in the attack. They were over the area almost before the last note of the siren had died and immediately the air was filled with a curious hollow, rattling sound. It was a sound which could not be localised or identified. It started in the distance and quickly grew louder and more intense until the whole sky was filled with it and the drone of the 'planes was subdued. "It was like the rattling of ten thousand dry bones" a resident stated afterwards, an apt description. Startled citizens staring skywards were not left long to wonder. Fires broke out all round them - and they knew that the unusual sound was caused by failing incendiaries.

Pembroke Dock was ringed with flame and the horizon was soon shimmering with bright, white, intense light. Inside the circle of fire the following formations of raiders poured their bombs with the usual lack of discrimination. The explosives were mostly of the smaller type and they fell on empty houses, in gardens and open spaces, and a few in the streets. But the town did not escape without paying a toll in life. The whole of the borough was deeply grieved to learn the next day that two lads of tender years, Arthur Kavanagh, aged 13, and Cyril Jenkins, aged 18, of Bufferland, both A.R.P. messengers, had been killed by blast. These lads, with the grand exuberance of youth, were energetically extinguishing incendiaries in a field alongside Bufferland when a stick of explosives fell right alongside them. A well-known resident, Mr. Jack Baskerville, High Street, was killed in the same area while helping his children out into the fields. The blast caught him but the children were saved. Down in Pembroke Street an R.A.F. man sacrificed his life to save his wife. The couple were hurrying to shelter when a bomb screamed down beside them. The husband threw himself upon his wife on the ground, was caught by the blast and killed. His wife, protected by his body, was uninjured, except for shock. On the Neyland side a house received a direct hit killing the four people in it - Mrs. Margaret Evans and her daughter, Mrs. E. M. Evans; Mrs. Esther Griffiths and her daughter, Miss Esther Griffiths.

When the siren sounded many people left their homes and hurried out along the Top Road, rightly or wrongly the practice of seeking shelter in cellars, etc., having become very unpopular since the May raid. There was quite a crowd on the road just outside Pembroke Dock when a bomb was heard - "coming straight at us" one of them said afterwards. The distant whine grew to a rushing, tearing

54

Heinkel ... The last big raid on Pembroke Dock - on the night of June 11th/12th, 1941 - was led by an elite Luftwaffe unit, Kampfgruppe 100, flying Heinkel He IIIs. This unit was the first of the so-called 'pathfinders', tasked with seeking out targets and marking them with bombs for other bomber crews to follow. They did their task well on Pembroke Dock that night, a night which is remembered as the 'fire blitz'.

Via Vernon Scott

screech and the frightened people threw themselves into the hedges and on to the road, sure that their last moments had come. The bomb landed plumb in the middle of the road but failed to explode! There were many other escapes just as lucky.

Watched from Pembroke, this raid was an awesome spectacle. Fire appeared completely to envelop the town, and through it dark clouds of smoke billowed and played. Every few moments there would be a bright flash against the red glow as the bombs exploded. The darkness above was broken by the golden, rippling stars of anti-aircraft fire and the dot-dot-dot of machine gun bullets as one 'plane after another tried to shoot down the barrage balloons which obstructed their path. The whole scene was a confusion of darkness and light and noise, awesome and well-nigh overwhelming. "Pembroke Dock is burning to the ground" was the word that went round, and no one thought it an exaggeration. After the phantasmagoria of the night people were surprised next morning to find Pembroke Dock so little changed. Traces of fire, of exhaustion, of tragedy there were, but the town still stood with no widespread havoc left behind by the vicious assault.

The Borough's fire fighting and A.R.P. services had again performed grand service. It is to them the credit must go for saving the town from destruction by flame. Helped by civilians, they extinguished innumerable small fires and dealt successfully with some big ones as well, including one in Commercial Row where a shop was completely destroyed and a number of houses extensively damaged. Those who were in the town described the raid as being as terrifying as any experienced, some being of the opinion that it was even worse than the attack on May 12th. There is no doubt that the number of casualties would have been higher had not so many people been sleeping out of the town, again proving the wisdom of the voluntary evacuation which was so much criticised. On the following day, the German High Command communique stated "Minor formations of the German Air Force last night attacked harbour installations at Pembroke on the Bristol Channel. Two large and three small fires were observed".

Apart from these two heavy raids on Pembroke Dock there were many small incidents in different parts of the county about the end of 1940 and the early months of 1941. Some sort of explosive fell near the Atlantic Club, Milford Haven, and a parachute mine in a field adjoining Snailton Farm, Dale, causing a crater twelve feet deep and twenty-four feet across. Another missile came down at Nolton without exploding while seven H.E.s fell in the Neyland area. One night in March several bombs fell in and around Pembroke Dock, but little damage was done. One raider flying low over the town met a terrific barrage and it later crashed into the sea near the coast. On many nights the whole county would feel the vibration of terrific explosions round the coast, mostly caused by minelaying aircraft dropping their mines on the rocks. April 8th was a night of much activity. Incendiaries fell in the Robeston Wathen district while at Caerbwdy, St. Davids, a 'plane, one of about a dozen flying along the coast, fired two machine gun bursts down a searchlight beam. There were no casualties. Explosives fell at Begelly, two residents receiving some burns. On subsequent nights incendiaries, bombs or mines fell in the districts of Saundersfoot, Carew, St. Anne's Head, West Blockhouse, Linney Head, East Popton and Pwllcrochan.

A sharp attack on Milton Aerodrome was carried out in the early hours of Tuesday, April 15th, 1941. Incendiaries were followed by a large number of small calibre H.E.s which caused extensive damage to the Y.M.C.A. building, the guardroom and sick bay. Several airmen were killed and others were injured. Some of the bombs dropped on the Sadgeston-Tenby Road, causing big craters. Outbuildings at Sadgeston Farm were damaged but there were no casualties. Incendiaries were dropped in Saundersfoot and two unexploded bombs near Carew Cheriton.

MILFORD'S MARVELLOUS ESCAPE

One of the most surprising features of the raids on Pembrokeshire was the way the enemy consistently refrained from attacking Milford Haven, probably the most important military objective in the county. Night after night the Luftwaffe flew over the area and, unless they were badly informed or their navigation was hopelessly at fault, they must have known that beneath them was a fish market handling large quantities of a vital food, a dock crammed with a variety of the little ships so valuable to the war effort, a town crowded with naval and military personnel, not to mention the flax factory and the mines depot nearby where a bomb in the right spot would probably have blown the place sky-high. As far as one is able to judge, there were one or two half-hearted attempts to bomb the mines depot but no real attack on Milford Haven ever developed.

The town's worse experience was towards the end of the summer of 1941 when an enemy 'plane sneaked in with a few Sunderlands returning to Pembroke Dock and after flying round for a while released a stick of four bombs which fell in the fields at the top of Priory Road. Two of the bombs straddled the road but no serious damage was done. On the same night a number of bombs was dropped at random around the south of the county but caused neither damage nor casualties. By this time Pembrokeshire had a fair share of anti-aircraft guns and countless searchlights and the raiders were given a hot reception and kept at a good height.

During the same week the quiet little village of Keyston, four-and-a-half miles from Haverfordwest, had a startling experience. Miles from any military objective and innocent of any war activity (except farming!) Keyston was the last place that expected any enemy attack. But that night early in September, 1941, a lone 'plane roaring along low in the dark sky dropped four bombs in fields sixty yards to the north of the village and in a line running parallel with the houses. The explosions rocked the village but, miraculously, no one was hurt and only minor damage was done. The only casualties were fifteen rabbits which were found scattered around the fields unmarked but dead.

This was the second time for exploding bombs to have disturbed the peace of Keyston. The first occasion was a few years after the first world war when on a Sunday afternoon, an aircraft - "one of ours", of course - developed engine trouble while flying in the area and jettisoned a few light bombs in a field near the village. No damage was caused apart from the small craters.

On the moonlight night of October 11th - 12th Tenby had its first experience of bombing. It had turned midnight when another lone raider spilled its bombs on the well-known resort with that senseless indiscrimination so typical of German airmen. Four bombs fell and one scored a direct hit on the house of Mrs. G. Thomas in Queen's Parade.

Sitting pretty ... This sizeable example of the Luftwaffe's bomb arsenal came down outside Milford Haven town in the late summer of 1940. Prior to being taken away - but presumably after being rendered safe! - it formed an unusual seat for Police Sergeant Fred James of Neyland and a naval officer.

Trevor James via Vernon Scott

Rescue workers rushed to the scene and found Mrs. Thomas lying dead in her bed. Her death created deep sorrow throughout Tenby and district where, a former Mayoress, she was one of the oldest and most respected inhabitants. Several houses were badly damaged and fifteen residents were injured. Again there were some remarkable escapes. The Civil Defence services worked splendidly in this their first real emergency, the Mayor (Mr. S. H. Hughes), himself a warden, setting a fine example. Rather ironically, Tenby's bombs fell in close proximity to houses where many Pembroke Dock people were seeking refuge from the dangers of their own town. "Nowhere is safe now", they complained next day but, generally, they accepted the incident philosophically.

Although the end of 1941 and the beginning of 1942 saw a steady decline in the number of attacks on Pembrokeshire, the sirens continued to wail night after night. "Jerry" was now paying more and more attention to our shipping and on innumerable occasions the warning would sound followed by the all-clear an hour or perhaps two or three hours later without even the distant hum of an aircraft being heard in mid-Pembrokeshire. Upon these occasions the enemy was strewing mines around the coast, the sea war being then at its height. Now and again, by accident or design, sea mines would parachute down inland and explode with terrific detonation. Upon one such night several mines fell in different parts of the county, including one near Camrose South School, another in Lambston and a third in the Spittal area, all of which rocked Haverfordwest. A white low-lying fog enveloped the county that night and it is possible that the German airmen, never too good at direction-finding, thought they were over the sea. Whatever the reason for such an unusual attack, the people of mid-Pembrokeshire spent a very unpleasant few hours. As each mine went off a bright red-yellow flash would fill the sky followed in a second or two by the explosion which sent a tremor through the ground for many miles around. People standing in the streets in Haverfordwest distinctly felt the blast of the explosives which fell near Camrose South School and Lambston. Although it was obvious to everyone that heavy calibre explosives were being used no one knew exactly what was happening and for Haverfordwest and district in particular, it was a night of much anxiety. But the morning's light disclosed surprisingly little damage and. thankfully, no casualties.

During one of these "ragged raids" at the end of 1941, a mysterious object fell through the roof of a house in Brooke Avenue, Milford Haven, occupied by Skipper Tom James. It was about two feet long and had a diameter of about six inches. As it crashed through the roof there was a detonation and damage was caused inside the house but when the object was examined it was found to be still intact. There were no markings on the casing and for a long time the A.R.P. people were mystified by the unusual object. Eventually, a Bomb Disposal Squad inspected it and pronounced it to be a 50kg. photographic bomb which had exploded.

THERE MIGHT HAVE BEEN FLYING BOMBS

One night in the early months of 1944 the Pembrokeshire sirens sounded in earnest for the last time. The Luftwaffe was on a widespread prowl, no doubt looking for signs of our impending invasion of the Continent, but they turned away without flying over Pembrokeshire. In some parts of the county, however, people experienced a touch of that empty feeling in the pit of the stomach so common in the troubled days of 1940-41. Soon after the siren had moaned itself out the sound of aircraft was heard but those who hurried to their doors were surprised - and somewhat relieved - to see navigation lights sailing across the sky at two or three thousand feet. They were "ours" returning from their patrols and a little later they landed at local aerodromes. But, although sirens were by now very few and far between, the whole county was tense and alert that night and during the short duration of the warning the Civil Defences were ready for anything the enemy could bring. When the all-clear went with no incident to report, no one thought it was the last time its sound would break the stillness of the Pembrokeshire night. On the contrary, there was a general feeling that this was the beginning of another throw, perhaps the last desperate throw, by the Luftwaffe. But nothing happened. Came the invasion of the Continent, the flying bombs, the rockets, and still Pembrokeshire remained undisturbed. Dire deeds by the once powerful Luftwaffe which were confidently expected after our invasion did not materialise. Local wardens, fire-fighters, ambulance drivers and so on, like those throughout the country, waited for the supreme test, but nothing came to the county. Men of the Royal Observer Corps posts dotted here and there in odd spots of rural Pembrokeshire stood at readiness for weeks, but had nothing more to report and plot than our own aircraft on their magnificent nightly tasks. With the capture of the Cherbourg peninsula and the falling back of enemy positions, Pembrokeshire began to breathe freely again. Even at this stage of the war however, the county was still in danger of aerial attack. Some U-boats had been fitted with V.I. flying bomb launching apparatus and warning of possible attack on coastal areas by this means was issued to defence organisations. But the general public was left blissfully unaware of this possibility.

The raids on Pembrokeshire followed the general pattern of those against the country as a whole. In the glorious summer of 1940 the winged monsters of the Nazi war machine roamed the skies without let or hindrance like a plague of deadly vampires. When winter came they made the nights hideous. Then, after the attack on Russia, the raids grew fewer and fewer until at last the sirens had to be sounded once a month just to make sure they were still in good working order! From the enemy's viewpoint the most successful attack on Pembrokeshire was the one which set the Pennar oil tanks on fire, but the worst raid against civilians was that on Pembroke Dock on May 12th, 1941, a date which will never be forgotten in that ill-fated town. That heavy raid came as a climax to weeks of non-stop night activity. Literally hundreds of enemy aircraft flew over the county those fine, clear nights before May 12th.

Going home ... Canadian airmen of No. 422 Squadron, RCAF, march to the railway station at Pembroke Dock in June, 1945. The war in Europe is over and their job for Coastal Command is done. The photographers on the left are positioned in front of yet another bomb site while on the right is a blitzed building. 'E.W.S.' meant Emergency Water Supply.

Dr. David Stewart

It was said "on good authority" that a secret instrument for counting aircraft at night, installed down about Merrion, broke down under the strain one night after registering over nine hundred! The "secret instrument" was probably some distracted member of the Royal Observer Corps, which organisation then only recently formed locally, was having a hectic time in the lonely posts about the county. No doubt the number of 'planes was also a slight exaggeration! Be that as it may, aircraft flew over regularly and in scores at the end of April and the beginning of May, 1941, and psychologically at least, prepared Pembroke Dock for its terrible ordeal on the night of the twelfth.

Pembrokeshire under fire produced a host of emotions, unknown qualities and unexpected heroes It was a period of distortion and exaggeration and lies, when the most innocent incident was apt to be most grotesquely transformed within minutes, and wild stories spread without the slightest foundation. An instance of this occurred early in 1940 when a man approached the writer in Pier Road, Pembroke Dock, with the information that the radio had just announced that Folkestone had been razed to the ground. The man, a complete stranger, said he had heard the bulletin himself. But it was a complete fabrication. Another instance was the announcement by the German radio that the "Pembroke rubber factory" had been set on fire! It was a period of mistakes and lack of co-operation, such as when the siren failed to give warning of impending attack, or the occasion when a lone.

R.A.F. fighter flying fast and low over Pembroke on a moonlight night met a wicked barrage from our own guns until its frantically winking recognition light stopped the attack; or the occasions when our anti-aircraft guns would roar into life and exploding shells would fill the sky although the sound of an aircraft, hostile or friendly, was nowhere to be heard. On the subject of mistakes, it is a fact that once in 1940 all the sirens in the county were put off without authority due to a simple mistake at the Post Office. As it happened there was a raid in progress at the time, so the sound of the warning was not exactly out of place, but having been put off without authority who was to say when the siren should give the all-clear? An hour later, long after the raiders had departed, a red message came through. Ten minutes elapsed and the "white" came through. The all-clear was given out to the centres and worried officials smiled again.

HUMOUR SURVIVED

It goes without saying that the period of the air raids was one of great trial and tribulation, when sudden death and senseless destruction went hand in hand sowing sorrow and despair. But, thank God, right through the sombre pattern the golden thread of good fellowship and humour ran firm and strong. Often in the midst of adversity some contretemps, some ludicrous incident, some witticism would lighten the grim burden of the day and, temporarily at any rate, there would be smiles all round. There is not an ex-Serviceman, ex-Home Guardsman or ex-Civil Defence worker who has not a fund of funny stories about the war; stories which, mellowing with the years, live clearly in the memory while details of sterner happenings fade and die. During the troubled months of the air raids there were more real neighbourliness, friendship and readiness to help those in trouble - and there were many - than Pembrokeshire had ever known before. This was typical of every blitzed area in the country and it is sad to reflect that with the restoration of peace and security the old aloofness returned. Humour came to the fore in a score of ways when the raids were at their height. There was a lovable Pembroke Dock character, later killed in an air raid who, whenever the siren sounded, would "hurry along through the blitz" even when no enemy aircraft came near the area! There were the inn-keepers who put up above the doors of their damaged premises such notices as "This House is More Open Than Ever"; the wags who said they wanted to use the

Sunderlander's view... From the rear turret of Sunderland P9606 of 201 Squadron, Canadian airman Steve Challen had a bird's eye view of the oil tanks fire. Steve always remembered his last flight in a Sunderland for this reason. His photograph is a poignant reminder of a dark moment in Pembrokeshire's recent history.

Steve Challen, DFM

bank vaults as shelters so as to be "in the money" before they met their end. Then there was the Park Street (Pembroke Dock) gentleman who, scrambling for shelter after a warning, shouted to his wife that he had had a stroke and could not move. A torch carefully switched on revealed that he had put both his legs into one leg of his trousers! A good lady in Gwyther Street dressing hurriedly in the dark on another disturbed night heard her dress tear apart up the back and concluded with, dismay that she was putting on weight. By the light in her cellar a few minutes later she saw that she had struggled into her husband's best white dress-shirt, now ruined beyond repair!

Wardens at the Pembroke Dock Report Centre had a momentary scare one night when, a few moments after the all-clear had set their minds at rest (temporarily anyway!), the air was split by an unearthly screech like a supersiren starting up in the next room. It was only Mr. Sid Phelps' parrot, recently rescued from Mr. Phelps' damaged home in Laws Street, saying what she thought about the war and conditions generally. Another scare was provided by Mr. Norman Grieve's car. Mr. Grieve performed yeoman service during those difficult days but unfortunately his car had a defective silencer and as he roared along the blacked-out streets on his mercy missions, more than one person was heard to shout "Look out, Jerry's machine-gunning the streets".

A leg-pull resulted in some strong language in Bush Street East one air raid night. Arriving for duty at the Report Centre, one of the wardens, himself an inveterate leg-puller, was persuaded that an incendiary bomb had just fallen on the houses opposite. He seized a stirrup pump and got to work, playing the water on the upstairs windows which happened to be open. A stream of abuse from the householder, wet through in his pyjamas, put an abrupt end to the operation!

One night during desperate efforts to extricate a gentleman from underneath heavy debris, one of the rescuers, Police Sergeant Bodman - recognised by all as among the bravest - was heard to say to the victim "Don't worry, I'll die here with you rather than give up". A little later, soaked through from his colleagues' efforts to extinguish a fire raging nearby, he had to leave to change his clothes. This caused one helper, Police Constable (later Sergeant) Joe Gough, to comment, not unkindly, "Well, he's determined to die dry!"

Another local well-known personality had his gallantry officially recognised - this despite the fact that it was known that on occasions he had hurriedly departed to reputedly "safe" places outside of Pembroke Dock after the sounding of the siren. "He was officially recognised for making the fastest time out to Bush Lodge", observer Constable Gough drily.

An unexpected clash of personalities against the background of the ruins of the May 12th blitz on Pembroke Dock provided one of those incidents which, although arising from the most serious circumstances possible, and in itself was a very small thing, was not without humour. It concerns, once again, the volatile Alderman J. R. Williams who, on the day after the heavy raid, was standing in Bush Street surveying the damage and denouncing to a small group of friends (including the writer) the alleged remissness of the county authorities in failing to provide adequate feeding arrangements for bombed out residents. Alderman Williams was in high dudgeon and was directing his criticisms mainly against

Aftermath . . . Oil tanks destroyed in the August, 1940, air raid were never replaced on the Lianreath site after the war. The remaining tanks were used by the Admiralty for many more years before being demolished finally in the mid 1980s. Today golf links mark the site where, in wartime, momentous events unfolded and many acts of heroism were performed. This photograph was taken in the early 1950s.

John Evans Collection

the then County Clerk Mr. W. E. Bufton, whose name he was using frequently and in no subdued tones. Just when he was being most uncomplimentary towards Mr. Bufton, the worthy alderman realised that a newcomer had joined the group and was standing at his elbow. He looked round - and there was Mr. Bufton! It was an awkward moment but "J. R." was in full stride and, unabashed, rounded on Mr. Bufton and exclaimed "So you're here at last. My name is Williams". Mr. Bufton looked at him steadily for a few moments and then, without a flicker of an eyelid, replied slowly and with shattering sarcasm "Not J. R. Williams?" The emphasis on the "J. R." was eloquent, for Alderman Williams' name was much in the news at that time as a critic of the County Council, and the whole essence of Mr. Bufton's brief remark was mock reverence at meeting the critic face to face. How this meeting developed after its inauspicious opening I cannot relate for the group broke up, leaving the two gentlemen to argue things out alone. It can be taken for granted, however, that Alderman Williams did not waste the opportunity of placing before the County Clerk a few "home truths" about the dire plight of Pembroke Dock people at that time.

Another incident, of an entirely different sort, comes to mind. It is not so much a funny story, although it has its humourous side, as a story of the stoic heroism of the ordinary man-in-the-street doing a part-time job in an auxiliary service, the Royal Observer Corps. Indeed, as an example of placing a strict interpretation of duty before consideration of personal danger it is almost unbelievable. Our hero was on duty at a coastal Observer Post in this county on a night when the enemy was busy mine-laying. Calmly for an hour or so he carried out the routine task of reporting by telephone the movement of the aircraft to the R.O.C. Centre in Carmarthen. Then, unexpectedly, he told the girl plotter in Carmarthen that he wished to speak to the Commandant. It was the middle of the night. The Commandant was at home and doubtless fast asleep. But our Observer was adamant; he told Carmarthen it was important and he had to speak to the Commandant. There were many comings and goings at the Centre and at last, albeit with great misgivings, someone telephoned the Commandant and told him the position. He contacted the Observer in his distant post at once. "What on earth do you want?" he asked. "Sir", replied the Observer "a mine has fallen alongside the post without exploding. I want your permission to leave"! Needless to say, he had his permission in double-quick time. Asked afterwards why he did not run as soon as the mine fell, the Observer replied, "Oh, there is an order which says we must not leave a post without permission". Thankfully, the mine did not explode and early next morning a Bomb Disposal Squad removed it.

Another example of coolness in face of imminent danger was provided by two Pembroke Dock police officers - the previously mentioned P.C. Joe Gough and P.C. Jack Evans. A small, unusual type of bomb fell in Argyle Street without exploding during the May 11th - 12th blitz. The two officers placed it in the back of the police car and drove first to a field near the railway station where they intended to bury it. On second thoughts they decided this might be dangerous. So they put the bomb back in the car and drove down to Hobbs Point where they threw it into the water. As they sighed with relief it went off with a big bang!

No one denied that the policemen had been exceedingly brave but, officially, all they had for their pains was a reprimand. They had moved a bomb without authority!

SECRET HISTORY!

The wonderful spirit of helpfulness and sympathy produced by the air raids was never more in evidence than during the days immediately following the May blitz. An Air Raid Distress Fund was opened by the Mayor, Alderman George Brown, and within a few days over £1,000 had been subscribed to it, £200 coming from Milford Haven where a meeting of businessmen was held to see what help could be given the stricken area. In the next week Milford's contribution alone rose to nearly £1,000 while Haverfordwest also sent a substantial amount, and there were many generous donations from firms and private individuals. But despite all the generosity, helpfulness and sympathy evinced about this time, the Mayor's Air Raid Distress Fund was inaugurated

Relic ... Half a century after the end of the war this Luftwaffe relic came to light in a display at Narberth to mark VE-Day. The 500lb bomb is believed to have been dropped in the Jury Lane area of Haverfordwest and thankfully failed to explode. It was made safe by Army personnel from Narberth and, 54 years on, went on public view as a grim reminder of the air raids made on the local communities. It is a prize exhibit in the collection of wartime items owned by Mr. Tommy Thomas of Commercial Garage, Narberth, who is seen in the photograph.

Gareth Davies Photography

with one of the noisiest and most discordant meetings ever held in Pembroke Dock – and that is saying a lot! The meeting was called by the Mayor who invited various people to attend. But four "uninvited guests" turned up – Revs. J. T. Morgan (Curate of St Patrick's, Pennar, and later Vicar of Pembroke Dock until his death): D. J. Phillips (Pastor of St. Andrew's Presbyterian Church, Bush Street); and L. R. Howells (Pastor of Albion Square and Trinity Congregational Church); together with Alderman J. R. Williams.

They contended that a meeting about such an important matter should be a public one. But the Major would not be outdone. He requested the four gentlemen to leave. When they refused, he changed his request into an order and, while tempers rose all round the room, the order became a threat that unless they departed the police would be called. Pandemonium broke and the Mayor, on his feet and with trembling finger pointing at the four gentlemen, repeated that he would call the police. A few minutes later, with the row still going on and the Mayor repeating that Alderman Williams must leave in any event, Deputy Chief Constable Thomas and a policeman arrived, as if by magic! With the sight of the blue unifrom and with a few sage words from the Deputy, the storm began to blow itself out and eventually it was agreed to co-opt the Revs. Phillips, Morgan and Howells and that Alderman Williams must leave. That irrepressible gentleman left – and at a meeting of the Council that night was reprimanded for upsetting the Mayor! But he was little dismayed, for a day or two later he walked into another meeting in Pembroke Dock, where heads of various departments in the county were discussing the position following the blitz, and made his presence felt before departing.

The story of the inauspicious opening meeting of the Air Raid Distress Fund was not told at the time although a *West Wales Guardian* reporter attended the meeting. It was feared that the publication in the Press of such undignified proceedings might have done incalculable harm to the fund and, consequently, to the suffering people of Pembroke Dock, and the *Guardian* decided not to report the meeting. Which goes to prove that the local Press at any rate is prepared to sacrifice good "copy" in the public interest!